MW01241431

# From The
# Outhouse
## To The
# Court
# HOUSE
*Secrets Discovered Along the Way*

# Jim Foster

# Contents

1. New Era in Dallas County  7

2. Growing Up in Poverty  13

3. Life Forever Changed  25

4. Lost Bucket of Gold  35

5. Trauma of Being Born Gay  42

6. My Introduction into Politics  59

7. Gearing Up for the Big One  66

8. The Big Shakedown  75

9. The Lost Son  86

10. The Inner Circle  93

11. Constable Scandal  100

12. Unconventional Defense Attorney  116

13. Loyal Female Associates  121

14. Not the Person I Once Knew  128

15. The Investigation Concludes  134

16. Overheard at the Courthouse  141

17. Agent Behind the Scenes  147

18. Preparing for Trial  156

19. Wrapping It Up  164

CHAPTER 1

# New Era in Dallas County

There is no easy starting point for a book like this. But let me begin with the day I was driving down Inwood Road in Dallas. Out of the corner of my eye appeared a vehicle that seemed to be tagging along. I would speed up. The driver next to me would also speed up. I slowed down and he slowed down. It was clear that something wasn't right.

Needless to say, I was concerned. You might have heard there are folks in Dallas running around with guns. Determined to learn who was trying to tag along, I gradually pressed on the brake. This caused the front of a tan Chevrolet Avalanche to pull up even with my passenger window. For several years at the courthouse, I had frequently parked next to a Chevrolet Avalanche—one that looked just like this. The thought of Commissioner John Wiley Price was messing with me flashed through my mind.

I thought, "Oh no, surely that's not JWP." As the vehicle continued to pull alongside, I finally caught a glimpse of a face. And yes, it was Price. Was he trying to intimidate me? Did he think

I was afraid of him? Those questions may never be answered. But I spent the rest of the day puzzled over his intentions. I thought about how he had intimidated others for years. Thought about the times he had threatened me.

Several friends had already asked if I was afraid of JWP. I always responded, "No, JWP doesn't scare me, but I hope the time never comes that he confronts me." I had always attended the annual county judge training seminar. On my return one year, a friend said, "I thought you had spent the week at a seminar." I quickly responded that he was correct. "Well, how did you get sunburn at a seminar," he inquired. "Oh, we spent the last two days on the gun range. Judges in Texas have a special license. They carry guns, even in the courtroom," I responded.

By the end of the day, I had reached two decisions. First, I felt that I should move away from Dallas. That was the most difficult of the two. After all, my roots run deep. I am a sixth-generation native of Dallas County, my great-great-great grandfather being a veteran of the Civil War.

The second decision was that I would write a book that provided little-known details about what actually transpired during my four-year term. That decision was not complicated. However, presenting those details in an interesting manner is quite difficult.

Perhaps we can fast-forward to the events that transpired right after my election. One of the news reporters mentioned that I would have an open-door policy. Anyone with a valid concern was welcome to stop by my office and discuss that concern. It was during my first week that someone walked in without an appointment. We shall call him Mr. Smith. He started off with, "Judge, I need to talk with you about the Bail Bond Board. Do you know who is on that board? Do you know that no one gets a bail bond license unless an under-the-table fee is paid?" he wanted to know?

Other items would follow, but my eyes were wide open. I began to connect the dots. I quickly began to see a very organized machine that operated behind the scenes. It was clear to me that the current district attorney was friends with Price. The state attorney general was not permitted to prosecute in Dallas County unless the DA invited him. I knew that would never happen. I also quickly discovered that the Texas Rangers depended on the Dallas County District Attorney to prosecute their cases. They would never offend a county DA.

There seemed to be no apparent answer. No viable solution. A thousand thoughts ran through my mind. On the way to the office the next morning, the search for answers continued. It was just as I neared the Triple Underpass that I finally decided to head back toward Oak Cliff, to my office on Bishop Street. Once inside my private office, I phoned the courthouse and let them know that I had an appointment that morning and would be in later.

My first call after that was to an attorney friend. We discussed calling the FBI and how that process works. FBI agents are not permitted to conduct investigations of elected officials without being requested to do so by the U.S. Department of Justice. So I made the phone call. About two days later, I met with Assistant United States Attorney for the Northern District of Texas Joseph Revesz and FBI Special Agent Dillon.

They made it clear that there would never be a meeting anywhere close to the Dallas County Courthouse. All meetings were in secret and at my private office in Oak Cliff. After a lengthy first meeting, I expressed my concern to Revesz. I told him that I was concerned that an investigation would never happen, that

Price had been placed on a pedestal and was untouchable. That's when Revesz leaned forward. He looked at me over the top of those horn-rimmed glasses and said, "You don't know how long and how hard we have wanted that man." I knew then that progress had been made that day.

Other meetings would follow, but always in secret. One of the agents always opened his briefcase just prior to the meeting. I wondered if he was checking to see if our conversations were being recorded. Several minutes later he would take another look inside that same briefcase. It was emphasized that I never let anyone know about our meetings. It was also mentioned that no meetings were ever to be placed on my appointment calendar.

One of the reporters for a popular weekly publication was soon asking questions and wanted to know if he could take a look at my appointment calendar. I deliberately avoided responding to the question for a period of time. He soon had a very negative article and reported that the county judge was spending time away from the office and refuses to share his calendar with the news media. I always wondered if word had leaked out. Were they looking for the bigger story? One that was sure to make front page headlines if ever confirmed?

But I never gave in. The news media continued to hound me. As time went on, Price became more and more vindictive toward me, especially after he discovered that I was against any attempt to sabotage the 5,000-acre Inland Port project. He even sued me, claiming that I had tarnished his reputation. My attorneys managed to stall the deposition for some time, which really angered Price.

Once the deposition was finally scheduled and underway, he became more and more angry. He claimed that I was not responsive to his attorney's questions. I'm not sure how he managed to pull off his next stunt, but Judge Ken Tapscott was presiding over the deposition. Once it continued, his attorney asked, "Judge Foster, are you investigating Commissioner Price?" I responded, "No. Not me, personally."

His attorney, then asked if I knew who was investigating Commissioner Price. I responded that I did. He then asks for the name of that person. I replied that I couldn't reveal that. Tapscott then stated, "You have to answer the question. You are under oath." The thought that Tapscott was standing up for Price even though he was clearly under federal investigation puzzled me. I will never understand how a judge could put his personal political future above a federal investigation. I responded, "The FBI." He then asked how many times I had talked with the FBI, and I responded that there had been several. He then wanted to know what questions they were asking. After a brief pause, I looked over at Tapscott. Without hesitation, he again instructed me to answer and reminded me that I was under oath. He then stated that I was required to answer the question. My response was, "Women. They want to know names of the women that Price is associated with." His attorney quickly changed the subject.

He next wanted to know how many times I had spoken to the FBI. As I glanced over at Price, he seemed to be experiencing pucker pains. I replied that it was several. "Well, then when is the last time you talked to the FBI," he asked. Now suddenly I realized the fertilizer was about to hit the ventilator. I paused. I looked down at my watch and replied, "About ten minutes ago." Price jumped up, banged his fist on the table, and said, "This deposition is over."

As mentioned earlier, the news media had not been very kind to me. But I could see this as an opportunity to turn things around. I realized that the deposition would become a matter of public record once it was transcribed and approved by the court. So, I made a phone call. Kevin Krause, longtime reporter with the *Dallas Morning News,* was very interested. He would walk over to the clerk's office every morning just as it opened. He was like a bird dog, constantly watching and waiting. He wasted no time getting a digital copy as soon as the deposition was made public. Now, for the first time it was factual. There was no more speculation. He asked me to keep it quiet and keep it away from the TV news media. He explained that he wanted the exclusive scoop on the story. I told him that I would keep it under wraps.

Early the next morning, there it was. Front page headline: "Commissioner John Wiley Price Under Federal Investigation." One of the reporters asked me, off the record, how long I had known about the FBI's investigation. My response: "Well, they had a microscope six inches up his rectum for two years before he even had a clue." It would be another four years before FBI agents arrested Price, and an additional four years before commencement of a trial. He faced eleven counts total. The charges ranged from bribery to tax evasion.

Price was more radical in the late 1980s. He and his followers threatened to take to the streets with M-16 rifles. He faced indictment at that time by the Dallas County DA for breaking a news reporter's leg. A *Chicago Sun Times* article quoted him as saying, "We will be in the streets, M-16s and all. It will be a call to arms." Of course, there is much more to my journey through those years. But perhaps we can gain some insight by first going back in time. Back to a period of earlier life and my deep roots as a fifth generation Dallas County native.

CHAPTER 2

# Growing Up in Poverty

Looking back at the days of my childhood, I now realize that we grew up in poverty. Neither I nor anyone else I knew realized it at the time. After all, everyone we knew was just like us. The entire nation was only a few years out of the Great Depression, and almost no one living out in the rural areas had a penny to spare. In fact, some had even lost their home, or the entire farm.

My maternal grandparents lived on the farm that provided a constant supply of milk, butter and eggs, but they depended on my paternal grandfather and his country store for their staples such as flour, sugar, coffee and other necessities.

I recall my maternal grandmother, Beatrice Merritt, on more than one occasion saying, "If it hadn't been for Al Foster, we would have starved to death."

And therein lay the problem. Almost everyone in those days bought their groceries on credit. And almost no one was able to pay their debt during, or immediately after the Depression. My grandmother, Eula Foster, had a thick ledger with everyone's name, items purchased and the amount they owed. I remember seeing that ledger, which she kept completely confidential out of respect to the families of their debtors. But she did reveal that the total owed was more than $23,000, which would be equivalent to about $500,000 today. Albert had money in the bank at the beginning of the Great Depression, but he came out of it broke.

He later revealed that only one man had paid his debt, and that was Ritchie Burst. Ritchie had bought a wagon load of corn on credit. When Al asked Ritchie how he was able to pay his debt, Ritchie responded, "Well, I always knew I'd be able to pay you back. I make good corn liquor, and people will pay for good liquor."

Life had not been easy for Albert and Eula. Both were descendants of early pioneer settlers in the Elm Grove area of northeastern Dallas County. His parents were G. W. and Emma Forster (Foster). G. W. arrived in the Elm Grove community in 1876. He, along with his mother, had traveled from Missouri to Dallas County in a buggy. After G. W. and Emma were married, they lived in a tent for over a year while their house was being built.

Their first child, Cora Mae, was born in that tent. She lived to maturity, but out of fifteen children, six would die during infancy. Remember, there was much less medicine in those days. Doctors were few and far between, and refrigeration had not yet been invented. The common cause of death is thought to have been what was known as "summer's complaint" which was caused from the lack of refrigeration for milk products. It was almost always fatal in children.

A solid row of identical tombstones identifies the place. Six of their infant children were buried near Sachse, Texas, at Pleasant Valley Cemetery. Pauline Foster, a granddaughter, once told me about the difficulty in getting grave markers for those children.

"There was no place around here to get headstones in those days. Grandpa Foster and Lewis Wells took the wagon over to Greenville, Texas, and ordered all six markers for those kids. A couple weeks later they took two dozen guinea hens on their trip back and traded the hens for those markers," she told me.

Three of their children married into the Wells family. Their youngest child, Mary Eva "Mollie" Foster, was born in 1900. At the age of seventeen, she found herself head over heels in love with Eugene "Ernie" Wells, a boy living on one of the nearby farms. Judging from some of the notes I read after her death, they were unusually committed to each other and married on April 8, 1917.

War clouds had been gathering when Ernie, along with about 40 other men from the Elm Grove, Pleasant Valley and Rowlett area of northeastern Dallas County were selected. This was the first Dallas County draft for World War I. Mollie was just devastated. She couldn't bear the thought of their being apart.

In those days the induction office was located in downtown Dallas at the Old Red Courthouse. After the new recruits were inducted, they would pick up their satchel and walk down Houston Street to Union Station, where they boarded a train. They were then shipped out to a military post for training. Ernie didn't know it at the time, but he would be going to Camp Travis at San Antonio.

Ernie's dad, Jefferson Davis "J. D." Wells, picked him up in a wagon to take him for induction. He and Mollie had been living at her parents' home. Just as Ernie started to climb up into the wagon, J. D. said, "It's a long trip into Dallas. You probably want to stop by the outhouse before we head over to the courthouse." The separation caused Mollie to grieve so much that she rarely got out of bed. Her frequent letters from home reached Ernie two to three times a week. The message was consistent. Her health was getting worse. Ernie managed to get a weeklong furlough. He spent almost every minute by her side, but her condition didn't improve. Ernie remained several days beyond his allocated leave. He had been at Camp Travis for almost a year and his unit was getting ready to deploy overseas. He received orders with written instructions directing his immediate return to camp.

Once again, J. D, picked Ernie up in the wagon, but instead of the courthouse, they were headed to Union Station. This time they stopped at the Central Wagon Yard, which was located near present-day Fair Park. While J. D. watered the horses, Ernie lingered and thought of the lonely days and nights without Mollie. He managed to get into the buggy, then turned his head away, choking back the tears. He withdrew the bottle of carbolic acid from his pocket and calling his father's attention to a passing car, he drank the poison. Wells turned to see his son at his feet. The wild dash of the city ambulance down Elm Street defied the laws of safety. Driver Fred Williams escaped accident and had young Wells on the operating table in Emergency Hospital in six minutes after his father gave the alarm.

Dr. V. P. Armstrong at Emergency worked frantically to save the boy's life, but in 15 minutes Ernie Wells was dead. "Don't for God's sake, tell them at home," pleaded the father with Dr. Armstrong. "They have only been married since war was declared," explained the grief-stricken father, "and she is only 19. The boy was called in the first draft, and she has grieved for him until we thought she is going to die," Wells pleaded.

Mollie, eventually recovered, but she never did remarry. She always lived at the original Foster homestead until her death at 91 years of age.

My grandfather, James Albert, did live to maturity. He married

Eula Ross in 1909 just one month prior to his 20th birthday. They were wed in the community of Happy Home, which was off the old road between Rockwall and Rowlett. The ceremony was performed as they both stood in a buggy with George Houston acting as witness. Not a trace of this community remains today.

Albert and Eula's first child, known as "Baby Floyd," was born about ten months after they married. He was a happy baby prior to meeting with a tragic accident. A local newspaper recorded the details as follows:

"Late last Thursday morning Floyd, the little sixteen months old baby of Mr. and Mrs. Albert Foster, was fearfully burned. He died a few hours afterward. Our information is that Mr. Foster, when at home, always did the milking. He was a little late rising that morning. He had promised to haul a load of hogs to Rockwall for his father. He asked Mrs. Foster if she would do the milking and that he would hurry on.

Before going to the cow lot, which was about two-hundred yards distant, she took the precaution to place little Floyd on the bed. Even gave him some playthings to keep him interested until her return. But he did not stay there, getting off the bed, it is presumed that he went to the stove. He then sat down under the apron and was playing with the fire, raking out some coals which fell on his clothing and burned them off him.

The fire did not blaze, but slowly burned the little clout from about his hips. The clothing on the upper part of his body was not consumed. Particles of the burnt clothing were found in each room of the house. It appears that he had evidently gone in search of aid. As the mother was nearing the house, she heard the unusual noise. She ran, pushing the door open, found the room so full of smoke that she could scarcely see. She ran into the different rooms of the house, finally finding the child in a squatting position in or near the corner of one of the rooms. She took him in her arms and started for help, screaming as she went. She had taken only a few steps when she was so completely overcome that she fell fainting with the precious bundle in her arms.

Some men picking cotton nearby had heard her screams and hurried to her side, but it was out of the power of man to keep its soul from taking flight. Funeral services were held by Elder Martin of Garland at the Cottonwood Church. The little body was interred in the Cottonwood Cemetery where an unusually large crowd of neighbors and friends attended the funeral.

While little Floyd has suffered an agonizing death, his little soul has been wafted to realms where there will be nothing but joy and happiness for him through eternity. Mr. and Mrs. Forster are among our most highly respected citizens and have the sympathy and esteem of all who know them. While this was an unfortunate occurrence, no blame can attach to either of the parents. They have our sympathy."

Al and Eula's second child was stillborn the following year. The loss was especially devastating for Eula. Carl Casey, their third child was to arrive twelve months later, on Christmas Day of 1912. Since there were no telephones in the area, a neighbor was sent into Wylie so that Dr. Brooks could attend to the birth. But the doctor was late, and Carl was already alive and kicking by the time the doc walked through the door.

Albert, like most other farmers and ranchers from the area owned a large section of timberland in the East Fork river bottom. The timber was primarily used for firewood, fenceposts, and Bois D'arc blocks used under the foundations of new homes, churches and schools. But Al had a mule-powered rotary saw that he used to cut the younger Bois D'arc trees into sections about two feet in length. He would then haul the wagonload of logs out of the river bottom and into Rockwall. The sections were loaded into boxcars of a steam engine locomotive and shipped off to government buyers where the logs were turned into dye for military's khaki uniforms.

Eula's parents were Samuel "Sam" and Elizabeth "Betty" Ross. Sam had already made several trips up and down the Chisholm Trail. He was driving cattle thru Indian Territory and on into Kansas when he met Betty. He later carried mail for the Pony Express. Samuel died on the front porch of their Elm Grove home as the result of a heat stroke in 1907. That was two years prior to Eula's marriage.

My mother, Dorris Merritt (1924–1998), was an only child, but she almost had a sibling about a year later. Her parents, Oscar and Beatrice Merritt, had gone into Dallas to attend the State Fair of Texas and left Dorris with Bea's sister. Oscar and Bea spent the entire day walking the fairgrounds before returning home. Bea had a miscarriage shortly thereafter. She placed the tiny baby in a shoe box, then walked out to the end of the garden where she dug a hole and buried the remains.

Times were difficult in those days, but life had to go on. Bea had learned responsibility at an early age. She had grown up in a family of seven children. Her mother wasn't able to nurse her, so her dad, "Papa," would hitch up the wagon and take Bea over to the Merritt homeplace where Mrs. Merritt would nurse her. Bea remarked in later life, "She probably wouldn't have nursed me if she would have had any idea that I would end up marrying her son."

Bea's older sister, Belle, had been doing the cooking during her childhood days after their mother had suffered a stroke. Bea explained how all of that suddenly changed one day. "I was sound asleep just before daylight one morning when Papa walked into the bedroom and called out for me to get up. Belle had run off and got married. I was only thirteen years old and didn't know the first thing about cooking, but I soon learned," she said.

Oscar was born at the old Merritt homeplace, which as of this day is still standing at the corner of Liberty Grove and Merritt Road. It is probably the oldest house in all of Rowlett. Robert N. "Bob" and Udorah Merritt built this house in 1896 and at least six of their eight children were born in that old home.

Their third child, Thomas was born in that house in 1896. He answered his country's call and was shipped off to France, where he was killed in action on September 26, 1918. It would be almost two years before his body was returned to the place of his childhood. Two days after the return of his remains, a funeral service was held in the living room of that old home as a crowd of neighbors and relatives gathered to pay their respects to the family.

R. N. Merritt (Jr.), along with his mother, traveled to the Rowlett area of northeastern Dallas County sometime after his dad was killed in Civil War battle during the siege at Petersburg, Virginia, on July 31, 1864. He married Udorah Flowers in 1890 and they built the landmark Merritt homeplace.

Robert N. Merritt, Jr. is probably the only person I ever recall meeting who was born in 1853. He lived in the old homeplace with one of his sons, Charlie Merritt and wife Clara. We lived about 100 yards up Merritt Road in a little small house that was part of the original Merritt farm.

Our dad had just recently returned home from World War II. He wasn't able to send his family a lot of money back then, since WWII soldiers were paid only $50 per month. Life was difficult for us in that little house. It seems as if the winters were colder then than they are now. There was an old kerosene heater in the middle of the room, and on the coldest of winter days we would be toasted on the front side and freezing on the back side. It got so cold one night that the water in the goldfish bowl was frozen when we woke up the next morning. Much to my surprise, the fish started swimming around once the water thawed.

There was an open cistern at the edge of the porch that was used to catch rainwater. I remember my mother out on that porch washing our clothes with lye soap on a hand-held rub board. I also recall our granddad Oscar showing up one day with a shotgun while we were playing on that porch. He was very protective of his grandchildren. There was a rabid dog nearby, so he hopped into his old green Ford pickup and drove about five miles down the road in order to protect his grandchildren.

I also recall venturing away from the porch one day and climbing down into an old water tank that had been mounted on a trailer. I was instantly under attack by a nest of bumblebees from the split second I entered that tank. The stings were so severe that I was paralyzed. My mother hearing my screams ran out to rescue me. She managed to escape without one sting. I recall her running across the yard and pulling me out of that water tank and I remember waking up several days later. I still was not able to get out of bed. Mother asked me in later years if I remembered getting into those bumblebees. I replied that I recalled lying in bed, unable to move. She then mentioned that she had some sleepless nights during that time. As I raised my brow and turned to look in her direction, she responded with, "The doctor told us that it was not likely that you would survive. You were stung over 250 times."

After I recovered enough to run and play, Mother explained that I was old enough to follow along the wooden planks and make my way to the outhouse when I need to "go." Being so young and so curious, I wondered why the adults needed all those big books in the outhouse. I soon learned that the correct name for those big books was the Sears and Roebuck Catalogs. I'm guessing they were not for reading.

There were four children living in that little house by this time. David was still just a baby. I remember watching my mother making his baby formula on many occasions. Hard to believe, but all the rage in those days was the bottle half full of Karo Syrup and the other half with evaporated milk. She would then place the bottle in a pan of warm water until it reached the perfect temperature, which was determined by squeezing a few drops on the underside of her arm.

Mickey Don was one year younger than I, and Darla June was two years older. The age gap was caused by our dad being away during the war. The three of us together thought there was strength in numbers, so we scooted under the fence and ventured about 30 feet out into the green grassy pastureland before we realized that an angry bull was headed straight toward us. You have never seen three little kids run so hard and so fast. We slid under that fence and ran into the house, where we hid under the kitchen table.

I don't remember when we moved into that little house on Merritt Road. I do remember standing out on the front porch one cold winter day when I noticed my grandmother Bea slowly approaching the graveled driveway in her white 1943 Ford sedan. I was barely five years of age. But I knew before she got out of the car that something was terribly wrong. Darla ran over to give her a hug, but she opened the front door and continued inside without paying attention to any of the grandchildren. Darla started to follow. I grabbed Darla's blouse and shook my head no before suggesting that we remain outside. In less than a minute, we could hear our mother screaming and wailing, "Oh no. Oh no. Please." We knew something was seriously wrong, but we didn't know what.

After he returned from the war, our dad earned a living by repairing automobiles. He had set up an auto repair shop on the north side of the driveway. He had gone into Garland earlier that day to get a few items. Just before leaving town, he stopped to put gas in the car and several additional gallons into a five-gallon metal container. The container was placed on the floorboard behind the driver's seat before heading back home. He headed out toward Rowlett on the ice-covered Bankhead Highway, which was the route from Greenville to Dallas. His car began to gradually pick up speed as he continued down the slight hill toward Dairy Road. This would have been on the outskirts of Garland back then.

A driver, in another car was unable to stop. She slid thru the intersection and Luke slid into the ditch. His legs were pinned under the seat. The gasoline behind the seat ignited and the entire car burst into flames. A flash fire roared throughout the entire car. Several bystanders could hear Luke pleading for help, but the flames were so intense they were completely powerless. The owner of the Garland News rushed to the scene from his office on the square. One bystander told him that he had to walk across the road in order to get away from hearing the pleas for help. He told the reporter that he probably wouldn't be able to go to bed at night without hearing Luke's voice screaming out.

A deputy sheriff arrived about twenty minutes later and a wrecker driver was summoned to get the car out of the ditch and the body out of the car. The wrecker driver asked if Luke Foster had been driving that car and the deputy sheriff explained that it appeared so. "Oh, God forbid. I know his family. He's got some little children at home." The deputy asked if he knew how to call the family and the driver explained, "No. They live out in the country. There are no phones out there. I don't know where he lives, but I know his mother-in-law. I'll drive out and let her know."

I was too young to understand exactly what was happening, but I realized that our lives were suddenly changing.

CHAPTER 3

# Life Forever Changed

As if in the blink of an eye, life would forever be changed. We could no longer remain in that little house on Merritt Road. We had no car, no telephone, no income, and no daddy. We were suddenly thrust into a much larger three-bedroom house with my grandparents, Oscar "Runt" and Beatrice Merritt on Elm Grove Road. Instead of an old kerosene stove, there were about three large Dearborn heaters located throughout the house. It was no longer necessary to fill up that one-gallon kerosene tank on the back of the stove several times each day. A large propane tank permanently situated out in the yard near the henhouse now provided fuel.

The house had three bedrooms with an exterior door in each that opened onto the wraparound porch. It may sound like a dream come true. But Darla, Mickey, and I were sleeping on pallets in the living room. David was just a baby. He and mother were in the middle bedroom, while Bea and Runt were in the front bedroom. Bea's elderly mother, Carah Pelton, was in the back of the house. I remember my mother crying right after breakfast the first morning we were there and my grandmother saying, "I just hope we can get through the funeral before that baby is born."

Most of the previous day had centered around contacting Luke's family. All of his five siblings, except G. W. "Dub," were off in other cities, and no one at Liberty Grove had a telephone. There was a lot of discussion about notifying his mother. She was just down the road, but Dub was concerned about how she would take the news, especially since she had lost her husband just a couple years prior. She had constantly worried about Luke while he was away during his tour of duty, not to mention that she had never really got over the death of Baby Floyd.

After having breakfast, milking the cow, and attending to the hogs, Runt cleaned up before he put on a starched dress shirt and a clean pair of freshly pressed overalls. Then, about nine o'clock that morning, he and Bea loaded my mother and us children into that white 1943 Ford sedan and we headed over to Williams Funeral Home in Garland.

Luke wasn't old enough to remember when Williams Funeral Home had brought their horse-drawn hearse out to the Elm Grove community. They picked up the body of his grandfather which had been laid out in the parlor of the old homeplace the previous day. His older brother, Carl recalled, "I will never forget that hearse pulled by those two solid black horses with shiny, silver-studded harnesses. It was ten miles into Garland, and it took them over three hours just to reach the house. There was an oval glass on each side of the hearse and we could see the coffin through the glass. All the men in the community lined their wagons up behind the hearse, and we went over to the

Cottonwood Church of Christ for the funeral. Of course Williams also did Papa's funeral, but they had a big modern Cadillac hearse by then. And now, I guess, they'll be doing Luke's funeral. That's three generations."

Cecil Williams came into the room where we were all gathered. He told Mother that he knew my dad. He even remembered how happy Luke was the day before Christmas a few years earlier when he stopped by and asked if he could borrow his ambulance the following day. Cecil said, "I will never forget asking Luke why on earth he needed an ambulance. Luke had a grin on his face that went from ear to ear. He told me that he needed to pick up his wife at St. Paul Hospital in Dallas. Then he added, "We got a new boy. His name is Jimmy. I need to take them out to see my mother. It's cold, the middle of winter and there is no heater in my car."

Cecil went on to explain that my mother needed to realize the funeral would have to be a closed casket service. That he had gone to the scene of the accident and saw the condition of the body, even before it was removed from the car. Of course, Mother was crying again after his explanation.

The following evening would be the visitation at Williams Funeral Home in downtown Garland where all evening there was a constant flow of people paying their respects. I knew almost none of the visitors, but I did notice Cecil Williams walk over to Carl and quietly speak to him about a black man at the back door of the funeral parlor. Cecil explained that it was Bubba Johnson, the longtime hired hand for Runt's brother, Bob Merritt. Carl instructed Cecil to send the man around to the front door. Of course my mother, Runt, and Bea immediately recognized Bubba and politely thanked him for stopping by to pay his respects.

The funeral would be at the little country church at Cottonwood the following day. I was too young to understand what was taking place, but I do recall being dressed in a sharp little jacket and nice shoes that day. I also recall getting out of the pew long enough to walk over to the coffin and run my hand over the velvet outer covering. This was the first time I had ever seen a coffin, and it would be many years later before I realized that this was a simple plywood coffin with a velvet textured wallpaper covering. It was the least expensive coffin available.

After the funeral, all the men and women would pass by the coffin. Some quietly looked over at us, and others seemed focused in another direction. It was the first time that I noticed the women kept their hats on inside the church, but all the men removed their hats immediately on entering. This practice really puzzled me. Once outside, all the automobiles lined up behind the hearse. We headed over to Mills Cemetery, which was located on the old Bankhead Highway between Garland and Rowlett. I don't recall anything about the burial service, but I remember being in the back seat of my grandparents' car. As I looked out the rear window, we were headed up a hill toward the cemetery. I will always remember the cars lined up as far back as I could see. I had never seen anything like it.

Jack McClain from Pleasant Valley and some other men knew that our mother needed money. They sent word that they would buy Luke's tools. He didn't have a lot, but I remember being fascinated as I watched him operate that chain hoist and a hydraulic floor jack. It wasn't a lot of money, but she needed every bit of it. A few days later she was on her way to the hospital where Charlotte Jane was born. She had almost enough money from the sale of those tools to pay the hospital bill.

Now there were nine of us living in that house. Yes, it was a grand ole house. It even had a large cistern that would hold an entire tanker truck full of water. There was running water to the bathtub and the kitchen sink, but no water heater and no indoor toilet. Water for the bath had to be heated in a teakettle on the kitchen stove. We were just like everyone else out in the country in those days. We followed the path to the outhouse when we needed to go.

It wasn't long before our great-grandmother deeded Mother a half acre of property about one quarter mile up the road. I'm fairly sure it was the best way to get six of us out of that house. To this day, I'm not sure who paid for the lumber, but I do know that several men from the community got together and volunteered to build us a house. That was a way of life in those days. The only person that I recall working on the interior was Bea's nephew, Donald Sperling. I have no clue how he knew how to build kitchen cabinets, but he did. Being young and curious, I had a lot of questions for him, and he always provided a kind and courteous answer. He was Frank and Nora Pelton Sperling's only son. They were just devastated a short time later when Donald died tragically. He had been plowing on the family farm when he decided to take a shortcut to another field. He was following the tracks across the railroad trestle when he was struck by a Katy Railroad passenger train near the East Fork of Trinity River bottoms. He was only 27 feet from getting off the bridge when he was struck. I remember attending his funeral. It was at the little Sacred Heart Catholic Church in downtown Rowlett. That was the first time I had ever been inside a Catholic church building.

Our granddad, Runt, may have been a farmer, but he was also an excellent carpenter. He oversaw the construction of that little house. And of course it was just like all the other houses in that part of the country. It had a cistern for storing water and a path to the outhouse.

We had our own house now, but our grandparents were within easy walking distance. We would visit frequently. I'll never forget siting out on the kitchen porch about a year after our dad's funeral. It was customary for the insurance man to stop by and collect the monthly premium in those days. Bea was just finishing up patting down a couple pounds of butter when he arrived. I have never seen anyone so insistent about buying a pound of butter. He started out at 75¢ for the block of butter and keep raising the price until he got to $2 which would be the equivalent of $22 today. My grandmother finally looked at him and said, no I can't sell it. I need it for those grandkids.

One day we were sitting out on the wraparound porch looking down toward George Nelson's blacksmith shop. I mentioned to my grandmother, Bea, about watching George Nelson pumping those bellows until he got a piece of metal red hot. Bea told me that George used to do a lot of things when he was younger. She then said, "He even made a wagon out of an old bois d'arc tree for Mr. Merritt. Bois d'arc wagons were very desirable in those days, since the wood wouldn't shrink up like oak and the other hardwood. He even made that rocker that you are sitting on and that butter mold and paddle I keep in the kitchen.

"You know, he's kin to you. He was named after your great-grandfather George W. Foster. Matter of fact, his mother, was the sister of G. W. Foster." I responded no, I didn't know any of that.

Then she continued, "You know that Papa was on the school board right after the old Liberty School and the Elm Grove School were combined. That's the Liberty Grove School right there by his house. Miley did the milking in those days, and George didn't like the fact that Miley could look across the branch and see the back of the boy's outhouse when she was milking. So he came up here one evening trying to convince Papa to get the boy's outhouse moved. Papa told him that he wasn't going to do it. The next evening George and Miley were back. They brought a two-gallon bucket of lard that they had borrowed, and George told Papa that he was returning what they owed and they wouldn't be coming around socializing any more. They walked back home and never visited again. I don't think they even went to Papa's funeral."

This went on for years, and then one night me and Runt were lying there in bed with the windows open when we heard a loud scream. We jumped out of bed and got dressed as quickly as we could before heading down the cotton row all the way to George and Miley's house. George Nelson met us at the front door and asked if we had heard Miley screaming. Runt assured him that we had and wanted to know if everything was all right and why she was screaming. George explained that Miley was having a stomachache and it seemed to be getting worse and worse, so she thought that she could ease the pain if she put some chloroform on it. But it looked as if she poured out too much and it began spreading everywhere until it reached a sensitive area. That's when she started screaming. "Now don't you be writing a book some day and mention any of this," Bea instructed.

I then changed the subject to the piano, since I was curious as to how someone living out in the country could have a large upright piano. My question was "Did you buy that piano in town?" Bea replied, "No I was just nine years old when a peddler came by here one day with that piano in the back of his wagon. He convinced Papa to keep it here for a couple of weeks, since it was getting late in the day and he wanted to get back into town before dark. I was just a little kid. I could barely reach the pedals. I never had a music lesson in my life. I taught myself to play. I could hear any song just one time and then play it. About two weeks later, that peddler showed up with his wagon and Papa told him to load it up. He said he couldn't pay for it and that's when I went to crying. Papas asked if he would take one of the milk cows for the piano and he left with one of our cows walking behind that wagon and I had a piano."

Our mother worked hard to provide for five children. I'm not sure how she learned to sew, but she made our shirts and Darla's dresses. Charlotte was born while we were staying with our grandparents. Bea took care of her so that Mother could work. As time went on, Runt and Bea seemed to get more and more attached to her, so she began staying with them at nights until eventually she was living with them.

Every Saturday, Mother would wash our clothes in a number 2 washtub out on the back porch. Everything was then hung out to dry on the clothesline. That same tub was brought inside the kitchen on Saturday night and filled with enough water for our Saturday night bath. No one wasted water in those days and that meant that the same bath water was used for each person. No one would consider doing that today, but it was a fact of life back then.

Having a birthday so close to Christmas meant that you never actually celebrated a birthday. It also meant that I wasn't able to start school until I was almost seven years old. We lived at the end of the line for the Rowlett school bus—the last house before it turned and headed back toward Rowlett. Mother took me to school the first day, but I rode the school bus from then on.

Darla, being two years older, was in the third grade by the time I started school. Mother had to make our lunch each day, since the City of Rowlett was not advanced enough to have running water or a high school. I don't recall if we stored the sack lunch in our desk or the lunchroom. There was a concrete reservoir with a pump on top that piped water to a drinking fountain that was out in the hallway.

About the end of the school year for second grade, several of the students were spending most of our recess time watching the construction of a water tower for the town of Rowlett. Some of us were fascinated watching this giant erector set take place right in front of our eyes. Once the tower was finished, anyone within the city limits could have delicious artesian water connected to their home. The city was officially incorporated in 1952 with a total of 250 residents and a land area of about two miles by two miles.

By the beginning of third grade, the lunchroom, with its long tables and benches, was gone. The two outhouses were no longer needed. We now had indoor restrooms attached to the new cafeteria with cooks and indoor gym. We thought were moving up in the world. But each student still had a wooden desk with a hole in the top for a bottle of blue ink. We were still using ink pens and were taught the art of writing with regular exercises.

It was about this time that Dallas County health officials discovered that the majority of children in the rural schools were not educated in oral hygiene. Most didn't even own a toothbrush or know how to brush their teeth. Remember, almost no one had running water. Most homes had a water bucket with a dipper on the kitchen counter. It turns out that county health officials were correct. A representative was sent out to all the rural schools with trained speakers carrying large flip charts and free toothpaste and toothbrushes. I'll have to admit, that I, along with the majority of the other students my age, had not been taught how to brush our teeth. But we sure learned that day.

Watching the erection of the water tower was one of the most exciting memories I have of school days at Rowlett, other than the discovery of mud balls and the cotton stalk by one of our classmates around 1952. The Christian Church adjoined the schoolyard on the west side with the Baptist Church on the east and a cotton patch backed right up to the edge of the schoolyard on the south side.

We had about 12 girls and 11 boys in the third grade. Just about every boy in the class was out on the playground one autumn day. It had rained just enough to make the classic mud ball out of the black gumbo soil. The dry and rigid cotton stalks made the perfect launching tool. I'm not sure which one of the boys—seems like it might have been Sherman Barber or James Earl Potter—soon discovered that a mud ball about the size of a golf ball could be attached to a two-foot section of cotton stalk. That mud ball could then be slung across the school yard where it would stick to the side of the schoolhouse.

Soon, just about every boy on the playground was slinging mud balls across the schoolyard. They laughed out loud as they stuck like glue to the side of that old brick building. One, or two, hit a window and a frightened teacher immediately notified the principal. I will never forget Mr. Ernest Hill, walking out on the schoolyard with that paddle in his hand. Just about every boy on that side of the building got a spanking that day. This was before pressure washers had even been thought of. Some of the mud was still there when school started as we entered the next grade.

CHAPTER 4

# Lost Bucket of Gold

Stepping back in time for a few moments, we can take a quick look at my early ancestors. They all arrived, walking, on horseback, or in a wagon pulled by horses, mules or oxen.

Harmon Newman, my fourth great-grandfather, was the first to arrive. His father, Thomas Newman, Jr., had been born in Georgia in 1792, but relocated to Mississippi where he served under General Andrew Jackson in the War of 1812. Thomas then relocated to Alabama and married Mary Sparks. It was here that Harmon Newman was born in 1832. Harmon later moved, with his parents, to the hills of Wayne County, Missouri, where Thomas purchased land along the Black River.

Thomas was no longer happy with the hills of Missouri after his wife died, so he sold the farm and asked Harmon to take him, along with a grown daughter, Elizabeth (Eliza) down south. He wanted to experience life in Texas. They slept in a covered wagon while a little log cabin was being built. That first cabin, with puncheon floor, homemade furniture, hearth and chimney made out of stones, sticks and mud served the three until a larger house could be built.

The three had traveled in a wagon pulled by a yoke of oxen in 1856. They settled on 57 acres of wild prairie land in an area that would later become known as Pleasant Valley (Sachse, Texas, today). This cabin served them well until lumber could be hauled from a sawmill in east Texas for a larger home.

Several other families had arrived in the area just prior to Harmon Newman. It was in the early fall of 1854 when a small group of Kentucky settlers prepared for their overland journey to the Texas frontier. The caravan of eleven covered wagons left Monroe County, Kentucky, and traveled first to Memphis, where it crossed the mighty Mississippi River and then on to Little Rock and finally over to Rowlett area.

The entire trip lasted forty-five days, with all eleven wagons arriving on November 1, 1854. It was later reported that "all arrived safely and without hostile encounters." This area had begun to grow rapidly, especially the area around what would soon become known as Sachse, where a saloon had been established.

Harmon Newman's dad, Thomas, had walked over to one of the popular gathering spots set up outside a saloon at Sachse late one Saturday morning. He was soon challenged to a fight. It would be a bare-knuckle fight. Thomas won the fight fair and square but soon accepted another challenger. He won that one also. Several more then took him on. He beat every man that dared challenge him that day.

But then, he was ambushed by several men on the way back home. His eyes were gouged out and he was left lying beside the wagon road (now known as Merritt Road) until being discovered by a Good Samaritan. He survived but was blind the rest of his life and depended on Harmon and Eliza to take care of him. He died in 1862. There was no cemetery in the area back then. The only burial ground in the area was the Kirby Family Cemetery at Rowlett. The body was placed in a homemade coffin. It was then placed in the back of a wagon for the five-mile trip to the cemetery, where family members gathered to dig a grave and pay their last respects to a family patriarch. This hallowed ground today is known as Big A Cemetery.

An event that occurred sometime around 2006, during my four-year term as Dallas County Judge, has caused me to recall another early settler to the area.

My office was on the second floor of the Old Schoolbook Depository Building across from the Old Red Courthouse in Dallas. As a matter of fact, I could look out my second-floor window and see the large white "X" painted on the street. It indicated the exact spot of President John F. Kennedy's limousine at the time of his assassination.

Cooler weather was just beginning to mandate a light jacket for outdoor activity on this day. My secretary buzzed me and indicated that one of the assistant Dallas County District attorneys would like to speak with me. The conversation started off, I thought, in a rather unusual manner.

Assistant DA: "Judge Foster, a matter has developed that requires us to know the exact location of Wells Bridge Road. It appears that none of our early maps indicate that there was ever such a road. Our research also indicates that you have previously written about Wells Bridge. Would you able to point out its location on this map?"

I was happy to point out its location. Then I explained that the road was probably never on a Dallas County map because it was primarily in neighboring Rockwall County. It only touched

Liberty Grove Road at the Dallas County line. This was always a dirt road and is now covered by the waters of Lake Ray Hubbard.

Back in the early days, travelers from the east that were headed toward Dallas would need to pay a toll in order to cross the East Fork of the Trinity River. Glover Wells had built a wooden bridge across the river and most tolls were paid in gold coins.

It was back in 1974 that I received a phone call from Foy Cross, the grandson of Miley Nelson telling me about his visit to the hospital to visit Miley. Foy went on to tell me about his conversation with his grandmother and the toll bridge. Here is what Foy had to say:

"You know that Mams (Miley Nelson) passed right after Easter last year. She told me something that I believe you need to know about and I think that you should go out to Liberty Grove and let Matt Wells know about it as well. Mams called me over to her bed side and in a very serious tone explained that Glover Wells rode his horse over to their house just before dark one night. He told me that he didn't want any of them kids to have his money. He had hidden two buckets of gold coins next to the well. He then rode back home and he died that night. I have never told anyone about this, but I want you to know. Mams died that night and I think that you should let Matt Wells know about this."

I assured Foy that I would make certain that Matt knew about the gold coins. The next day I got a call that Matt had died the day before. I immediately called Foy and told him that I think it was best if we didn't tell anyone else. It seems as if they all end up dead. Foy remarked that he wasn't sure that any more of the grandchildren were still living. Even if one could be located, it was probably best not to let them know.

A few years later I stopped by to visit Hubert Raney at his little home on the corner of Rowlett and Chaha Roads. I ask

Hubert if he had ever heard of Wells Bridge. Then I noticed a grin, from ear to ear, instantaneously appearing across his face.

"Yes, Grandpa Raney paid 25 cents to cross that bridge. He left his home in Tennessee at the age of sixteen. He walked all the way to Liberty Grove. He complained for twenty years about having to pay a full day's wages just to cross that bridge. He would tell me about seeing wild deer roaming the area. It was right across the road from where we grew up. You may not know this but Glover Wells owned that bridge. His old homeplace was right across the road from where we lived."

I responded with no, I didn't know that. Then I mentioned that I had intended to tell Matt Wells about the "lost gold." But before I could get another word out, Hubert replied, "If he were still living, there was no need to tell him. Back when I was just barely a teenager Matt and Charlie Warren would stop by our home at least three times a week. They always showed up around breakfast time. My mother would put a couple extra sausages in the skillet and add a little extra milk to the gravy.

"Just as we sat down to eat a big breakfast of sausage, eggs, biscuits, and homemade gravy with some mustang grape jelly, Charley would always start in with 'I had a dream last night about where that gold was buried.' It always started off with how many paces it was from a certain tree. He and Matt, both grandsons of Glover Wells, would then go out and start digging right after breakfast.

I walked up the hill about halfway between our home and your Grandpa Al Foster's home one morning and found them down inside a hole they had dug. It was over six feet deep. They never did find any of that gold.

The last time I saw Hubert would have been in early 2009. He had requested my help in locating a live-in helper due to his failing health. His wife had died in 1981 and Hubert's health was rapidly declining. I placed an online ad and Hubert narrowed the field down to three applicants.

I called Hubert the next morning and inquired if he had made a decision. He responded with, "Yes, but she wants cable TV in her room so she can watch her stories." I explained that he should order the cable TV then. Hubert, replied, "I tried to, but they want a credit card." Of course, I immediately suggested that he give the cable company his credit card number.

Hubert promptly responded with, "I can't. I've never had a credit card. I always paid cash." When I ask if he would call the bank and order a credit card. Hubert replied, "I called the bank and that young man that I talked with told me that I couldn't get a credit card because I have never had a credit card." Of course, I immediately wanted to know the name of that young man.

Within just a few minutes I was on the phone to the bank in Rowlett and ask to be connected with this young manager.

"Roger, this is Jim Foster, Hubert Raney's cousin. He asked me to call you because he was asking for a credit card and tells me that you declined to issue him a card."

Roger quickly responded with, "That's right. Mr. Raney has never had a card and, therefore, our guidelines do not permit me to issue him a card."

I wasted no time in asking Roger if he knew the bank manager and he quickly explained that he did. At this point, I said, "Roger, I want you to go in there and tell the manager that Mr. Raney has asked me to bring him over to your bank tomorrow morning so that he can withdraw all his money."

The next morning, I phoned Hubert about nine o'clock in the morning and ask if he had heard from the bank. In an excited voice, he replied, "Oh yes. They was knocking on my door at

8:30 this morning with my new credit card."

Hubert never got to use that card. He died while leaning back in his living room recliner just a few days later.

I was living in the Oak Cliff section of Dallas by this time. Several of the old-school politicians had become friends. The legendary Dan Eddy, retired justice of the peace, was part of that bedrock group. Oak Cliff was completely different in those days. It was more like a small town that had been swallowed up by the big city.

Dan Eddy, his wife, and I were at dinner one night when he began recalling some of his previous encounters. I'll never forget his telling about the bailiff rushing into his chambers. The bailiff was all excited about a woman in the courtroom. He blurted out, "Judge, there's a woman out there with a gun in her purse. Do you want me to take care of it?"

"No, you go out there and get 'em ready (call the court to order). I'll be right there. I'll take care of it," Eddy replied.

The bailiff returned to the courtroom and announced, "All rise." Judge Eddy walked into the courtroom. He promptly gave the gavel two loud bangs. Then in a loud and stern voice, as if over a public address system, he intoned the following warning: "Now I hear there is a woman out there with a pistol in her purse. You come forward right now, or you will spend the night in jail." Six women came forward, he told me.

CHAPTER 5

# Trauma of Being Born Gay

Neither being born into a life of poverty nor losing my father at an early age was particularly traumatic. After all, my father had been off fighting a war for the majority of my life. We grew up out in the country with grandparents, aunts, uncles, and cousins scattered all over the community. They cared for us just like we were their own. But growing up gay was different. It was the most difficult aspect of my life.

By the time I reached six or seven years of age, I realized that this was the way I was born. I remember sitting in the back of our green Chevrolet coupe. It was late one afternoon. We had pulled up next the old schoolhouse at Rowlett. An attractive lady walked by and one of the men in the front seat replied, "Wow. Look at her. Now that's some mama." I immediately wondered why they didn't talk about the men that way. After all, I thought some of the men were quite handsome. I grew up wishing that I could change my feelings. But it never happened.

Those emotions seemed to especially torment me as I grew older. By the time I was sixteen, I felt the need to talk to someone about these feelings. But there was no one around that I felt comfortable talking with—no one that wouldn't condemn me for being the person that I was. The first sign of a new harvest moon would always draw me out into the cotton fields. I felt as if I could at least talk to God. Perhaps God would answer my prayers. So, I would walk up and down those long rows of cotton talking with God. Hoping that my voice wouldn't carry through the night skies. Hoping no one at home was standing out in the yard listening. Hoping that only God would hear me and praying that I would be changed. I would beg God to change me so that "I could be like everyone else." Those prayers were never answered.

I'm not sure why, but my mother felt responsible. I will always recall her suddenly bringing up the subject one day when I was around sixteen. Out of the blue, she mentioned, "It is my fault that you are the way you are. I'm going to talk to the preacher about this." She never brought up the subject again, and I have no clue as to why she felt responsible. We grew up attending the Church of Christ. It was a small country church, one that got its start on the old Wells Bridge. This was back when they held all day Sunday services with dinner on the ground in the late 1800s.

The following Sunday, the preacher brought up the subject, but all that he said was "I've been asked to address the subject of men and women. I have searched the scriptures from one end to another. There is no place in the Bible that I find where it says that we must be married."

This was about the same time I entered high school in the small nearby town of Wylie. I was soon having strong feelings for another country boy. This was during the time that homosexual conduct in the state of Texas was illegal. Everyone knew that back in those days, and neither he nor I ever discussed the subject. He did drive out to Liberty Grove to visit me one day during summer break. It was an awkward visit. Neither of us had the courage to ever bring up the subject. I always thought it was because of his strong connections to his Baptist upbringing in one of those little country churches.

I graduated high school during the height of the Vietnam War. It would be another two years before I received that notice in the mailbox. In big bold type appeared: "Greetings from The President of the United States" printed across the letterhead. They gave me thirty days to get my business in order before reporting for induction.

My departure was in a DC 3 turbo prop plane from Love Field Airport at Dallas. Then it was on to Fort Polk for basic training. After basic training, and additional specialty training at Fort Rucker, I was back on a turbo prop plane at Love Field and headed to Fort Eustis, Virginia. When I looked up, there was my high school friend in his military uniform. We had a brief conversation and he told me where he was headed. The plane made only one stop and he was the only one that got off. He was just standing out on the runway. Soon a military jeep drove up. He threw his duffle bag into the back before hopping aboard their ATV. We then continued on for a short distance to Ft. Eustis.

I was soon assigned to the training department of Headquarters Company. Even though curious, I never dared to discuss the subject of sexuality with anyone in those days. This was during the time that you could receive a dishonorable discharge from the military if it was thought that you were gay.

I'm not sure how, but I managed to scrape up enough money to buy an old 1954 Ford. It was not much of a car. But I was one of the few troops in the company with a car of any kind. Earlier in the day I had overheard some talk around the barracks about a club in town called the Wharf.

We didn't have Google in those days. So I managed to discretely look through a phone directory until I found a listing with the address. That weekend I drove around town until I located the place. I completely expected to walk into a group of perfect strangers. Then to my surprise, there sat our company commander. I immediately thought that a sharply dressed handsome man like him was strictly in the place by accident. After all, he drove one of those expensive collector type Corvettes. He loved watching heads turn as he drove slowly down the street in that vintage show piece.

The commander soon recognized me. After all, my office was just across the hallway from his. He motioned for me to come over to his table and we soon engaged in conversation. It wasn't long before he invited me to his quarters which was off post. I spent the next twenty minutes trying to convince him why I thought this was not a good idea.

Newport News must have been a small town in those days. My name was never mentioned. But, by nine o'clock that Monday morning I could hear a sergeant ranting and raving. "That f----- q---- captain was at the Wharf again over the weekend. I will see to it that he is shipped out to Siberia." A week later we had a new company commander. I was relieved that my name was never brought up. But the resentment was abundantly clear.

Once my two years of service ended, I headed back to Liberty Grove in that old 54 Ford. A friend was getting discharged at the same time and would ride with me to Dallas in order to save money on his airline ticket to California. Once we got to Alabama, I said, "You are not going to believe this, but my great-grandmother just passed away." He responded with "You could not possibly know that."

I pulled off the main highway and drove around looking for a pay phone. Then I asked the operator to make a collect call to my grandmother's house. Her sister answered the phone. I asked, "What are you doing there?" She responded, "We are waiting for someone from Williams Funeral Home to get here." She then asked why I was calling. I told her that I was in Alabama, but somehow I knew. Then I asked her to tell everyone that I would drive through the night and I expected to be there sometime the next day.

Finding a job that I was happy with in those days was difficult. I discovered right away that I did not like mixing dough in a large bathtub. My tenure with General Mills was short lived. I was soon driving all the way to Grand Prairie, Texas, every day where I was trained in aircraft electrical systems. I had a short career with LTV. My big problem here was just standing around waiting for something to do. I wanted to feel as if I was contributing. I soon found a job at SPACE Corp. in Garland, a company that specialized in building test equipment for military jet engines. They also built Mormon Trucks. I used the knowledge I had gained at LTV to easily qualify for the job.

In the meantime, some relatives came to visit my grandmother Beatrice. One of those visiting was her nephew. He was a former Garland champion tennis player. I had heard about Barry Pelton for many years. This would be my first time to meet him. Barry told me that he had accepted a teaching job at the university in Baton Rouge. He also told me that he had bought a house there and had ordered new furniture from Sears and Roebuck. I ask Barry if it would be okay for me to drive up for a visit. He assured me that it would be all right. He then introduced me to his friend and told Mike that I would be coming to visit them soon.

After everyone left, my grandmother and her sister Nora began to talk. Nora told about a trip out to San Francisco to visit Barry. I knew then that there was finally someone I could talk to about gay life, someone that would understand and could explain to me about the real world.

A week later I showed up at Barry's new home. His furniture had not yet arrived. That night we slept on pallets on the floor. The next morning after coffee, I told him that I had a few questions. Then I explained that they might be personal. He assured me that it was okay. He then reminded me that, after all, he was a PhD.

I'm not sure why, but that seemed to make me feel better. It was difficult for me to understand how Barry could be so comfortable with his life, and I on the other hand was very concerned about the retaliation from others. He quickly explained that those were valid concerns and that I should find a way to relocate to a larger city. It would be years later, and after his death, before I discovered that he was also the victim of bias and prejudice.

He also told me that I need to understand that being gay is perfectly normal. As time went on, I did move into town, but making gay friends took some time. A few gay bars were beginning to spring up in various locations across Dallas. This was in the late 1960s, and it was not uncommon to hear about police raids during those days. Just touching another man could land you in jail back then.

About a year later, I met a handsome, blonde man straight from the ranch in Brady, Texas. We became very close friends. He would bring tears to my eyes as he told about attending the academy for the Texas Highway Patrol. After graduation, he was assigned to an area near Austin, Texas. He went on to mention that he was up for promotion. The department conducted covert background investigations in those days. His home was placed under surveillance. It was soon discovered that he had a roommate. They even noticed that the two were sleeping in the same bed. He was immediately fired. He never got over that. He said that when he officially became a state trooper, it was the first time that his dad had ever told him that he was proud of his accomplishments.

I was living in Garland by this time and working at SPACE Corp. I seemed happy with my job. It was rewarding in that I was one of the few employees in the company that understood the electrical system on those Mormon trucks. These trucks were all custom order and one of a kind.

It was during this time that I had met a new "friend." After a few months, or so, I asked him if he would like to spend the weekend in Baton Rouge. He agreed, and early one Friday evening we headed out in my Nash Rambler. It was while we were standing out in Barry's front yard the next day that we decided to become partners.

A longtime employee of a division of Johnson & Johnson in Arlington had called the shop foreman at SPACE. He said they were looking for someone with electrical knowledge that could be placed in charge of a new product. The foreman asked if I was interested. The answer was "Of course." I was always looking for new adventure, so I accepted the offer. This required that we move to Arlington.

Our relationship was kept private. I advanced rather quickly with the company. My partner had back surgery about six months after our move. It was impossible in those days to get a job after back surgery. I had been with the company for about five years when he convinced me to see about getting him a job there. It was the biggest mistake I ever made.

*Jim Foster, about 1978 at Johnson &
Johnson plant, Arlington, Texas.*

Employees began to talk, and upper management began to question me. One of the vice-presidents even came to my home on a Saturday afternoon with a lame excuse to walk through the house. Then he asked, "Do you have anyone living with you?" I responded no, which was true. My partner and I had already decided that he should rent an apartment for that very reason. Nothing looked out of the ordinary, and the VP stood by me for the next couple of years before his retirement. The day after his retirement, it started all over again. It was clear that their religious prejudice would reign above all else.

The Arlington J&J company was combined with a J&J company out of New Jersey about this time. I could see the writing on the wall. I resigned and started my own company. The J&J facility at the Arlington location closed a few months later, and the operation moved to Malaysia. My partner and I had already separated by this time. He remained in Arlington, and I moved to Dallas. It was a difficult separation, since we had been very close, and he was close to my family back at Liberty Grove. It would be over a year before I saw him again. I had stopped by the Farmers Market one Saturday afternoon when he appeared at a distance.

There was no question in my mind that it was he. This was during the early stages of the HIV epidemic, and he looked as if he had lost a lot of weight. I never went over to acknowledge his presence, and I don't think he was even aware that I saw him. But if you got sick in those days, you almost never lasted more than three to five months. The vast majority of my close friends died during this time. I stopped counting after the number reached twenty.

The father of one of my close gay friends was a doctor. You would think that because he was educated, he would understand. The truth is, he never forgave his son for being gay. He didn't even want any of his close friends in the hospital room during his son's last few days as he struggled for his last breath. The mother of another close friend told me that it was okay to visit, but please keep it a secret.

There was a gay church near my home that I was attending every Sunday. The epidemic hit this little church especially hard. There was at least one funeral almost every day. The preacher and the staff were especially strained. And then the KKK announced that they would be visiting this church on a certain Sunday. The minister met privately with the church leaders prior to their arrival and told us that the service would open as usual. Then there would be a song. He would then step forward and invite everyone to hold hands for a prayer.

The service started and everything went according to plan until it was announced that we would be joining our hands and our hearts in a word of prayer. That's when about a dozen members of the Klan jumped up and ran out the back door. They were followed by several undercover officers from the Dallas Police Department and joined outside by local news reporters. To my knowledge, the group never returned.

After starting a small alarm company and selling my home to the district manager for Montgomery Ward, I landed right in the middle of Oak Lawn. This was considered the gay district of Dallas in those days. My theory was that I offered a unique service for the gay homeowners.

Business was slower than I had projected, and times were difficult. I will never forget walking into a Tom Thumb supermarket with 76 cents in my pocket. I wandered around the store searching for my best dinner option that night. But I survived, and business began to gradually increase. I became known as the man that provided security service for the gay community.

About eight or nine months later, I received a call from Frank Caven, a legendary owner of several gay clubs. Frank wanted me to meet with him at his Turtle Creek office the next day. I showed up at the appointed time, thinking that the meeting would be about security systems. But Frank wanted to talk about his customers being attacked on the streets. "Some attacks even take place as they cross Throckmorton Street going from one club to the next," he told me. I explained to Frank that I provided security systems and not security service.

Frank was older and wiser and had years of business savvy under his belt. He looked me square in the eye as he said, "Here's what I want you to do. After dark tonight, I want you to observe our customers as they cross Throckmorton. For thirty minutes. Just thirty minutes. And I want you to meet me back here tomorrow at this same time. We will discuss your observations."

I agreed and reluctantly made my way over to the intersection of Cedar Springs and Throckmorton Streets at the appointed time. Young men were crossing the street, but none seemed to be in any danger of any kind. After all, this was a well-lit, major street in Dallas, Texas. Then suddenly a large man rushed one of the young men and yanked the gold chain from his neck. About five minutes later another young man was hit in the head before his gold necklace and wallet were removed. Five minutes later, the ritual was repeated near Throckmorton and Dickason Avenue.

Needless to say, I didn't get much sleep that night. My mind seemed to be turning back to the days of my youth and the time that I spent with my uncles, Barney Foster and Garland Murry as they taught me to hunt. A few minutes later I was thinking about my military training and the marksmanship badge that I proudly wore during my years of service. I also thought about my combat and survival training. My mind seemed to race all through the night. After tossing and turning all night, I finally fell asleep, just as it was time to get up and make coffee.

Frank started off with, "I saw you out on the street last night and I know you witnessed some unpleasant activity. So, tell me what you think. Will you help us out? It would be a great service to the community. I don't want an outside agency in here. They wouldn't understand our situation and the police department wants to arrest our customers if they are called. We don't even contact them anymore."

I told Frank that I would provide the service, but first I needed to modify my license so it would include on-site security service. I also needed to arrive at an hourly rate. Then I assured him that I would get back with him in a couple of days with the final details. This would have been about 1979, and I would provide that service for the next twenty-five years. It was discontinued once I was elected Dallas County Judge.

As time went on, the area became more and more violent. My employees were soon armed. I spent many nights until two o'clock in the morning out on the battlefield, only to get up early the next morning devoting my time to the daily operation of the alarm company. One of my employees was especially traumatized after being the first on the scene of three murders within one month. The third murder was of a young man who had just gotten off duty at Hanky's Hamburgers on the corner of Throckmorton and Cedar Springs. He had walked to his car, unlocked the door, and was starting the engine when he was shot and killed because he wouldn't open the car door.

Another senseless murder had taken place at this same location about two weeks prior. The victim was a young European college student who had arrived in the country only a few hours earlier that day. He wanted to experience the area firsthand, and some friends dropped him off near the clubs. Two minutes later he lay dead in the middle of Throckmorton Street. The perpetrators were eventually apprehended and revealed that this was their initiation into one of the many ruthless gangs operating in the area.

One of my younger security officers walked up on three Mesquite High School students. They had one of the customers down on the ground and were taking turns hitting him in the head with a baseball bat. He apprehended one of the perpetrators. Two other security officers chased the other two, but they got away. Paramedics and Dallas Police were called to the scene. As the apprehended leader of the group was being placed into the back of a squad car, his two partners in crime returned to the scene. After a brief foot chase, they were also placed into custody.

Times were beginning to change, and all three were convicted and served time. But prior to that almost no one was convicted of a crime or served time for causing seriously bodily injury to a gay guy. About six months prior to this, I had personally witnessed a customer from a straight motorcycle club walk up behind a young man and bust the back of his head open with a beer bottle. About three weeks later, I received a call from one of the assistant district attorneys. He told me that there would be no charges and the case was being dismissed because the victim had propositioned the attacker. I explained that I was there, and it didn't happen like that. "Well, this guy has a pretty good attorney, and we don't believe there is a case here," he told me.

The police department had assigned to the area a sergeant who wanted to work with the community and finally bring some trust between the department and a community that was beginning to get somewhat organized. One of his patrol officers followed one of my security officers home one night and explained that he would like to be in a relationship with him.

This reminded me of the time that our company commander invited me over to his off-post living quarters. The patrol officer kept insisting and the next day my employee phoned the patrol sergeant and asked if he would speak to the officer. He emphasized that he didn't want the officer in trouble, just stop pursuing him. The sergeant promised to take care of the situation. It appeared that progress was finally being made. But within hours, the chief of police sent word for the sergeant to appear in his office.

The meeting started off with, "Sergeant, as you know phone calls are recorded and monitored. We have reviewed your call about the patrol officer and his attempt to get a date with that queer security officer. You need to fire him before his shift starts tonight." The sergeant responded with, "And if it were a female that he was trying to get a date with would he still be fired, or would you give him a two-day suspension?" The response was "You either fire him or turn in your resignation before the day is over." The sergeant resigned, and they fired the patrol officer that same day. Many of my friends know the sergeant. Therefore, he will remain anonymous. But I will forever owe him a debt of gratitude for standing up for what was right.

A short period later, it seemed as if the Oak Lawn community was once again making progress. I was speaking at public events about how to keep safe while in the area. We even had had two gay city council members elected and it felt as if we were moving forward. All of this seemed to fall on the heels of the HIV epidemic, and any progress that had been made was suddenly pushed back for another twenty years. HIV drugs were virtually impossible to obtain and some of the local leaders set up what became known as the Buyers Club. A movie was even made about the experience in later years. I guess my "Christian upbringing" kept me alive through all this time. Some of my cousins and many friends were not so lucky.

I wanted to save everything else related to being elected and serving as Dallas County Judge for later in the book, but one item should be told here. It all started after a trip to Brazil in 2011. It was sometime after that trip that a dark spot showed up on a lung x-ray. An MRI with contrast proved that something was there. A specialist told me that it was on the back of the upper left lung and required removal of a rib in order to perform a biopsy. He also advised me that it would probably be better to just remove the entire upper left lung.

I was scheduled for a routine consult on the day prior to surgery. The doctor looks at me and says, "I see here that you have named your partner as the primary contact." I quickly informed him that was correct. "Are you in a monogamous relationship," he asked? Yes, I replied. Well, you need to go by the lab and get an HIV test before you leave. The test was negative, and the surgery took place the next morning. But there was a problem. I stopped breathing during surgery and they felt it was necessary to wake me up while I was cut open. My friends later told me that they could hear me screaming all over the hospital. Internal bleeding caused an emergency late-night operation a few days later.

I began to wake up the next morning while in ICU. I thought I was dreaming at first. There was a vision of an African-American woman sitting in a chair across from my bed. Just as I opened my eyes, she began to speak. I had already pressed the nurse call button. This lady started out with, "Mr. Foster, I am with the Dallas County Health Department. I used to support you before you got crossways with John Wiley Price. Now, it looks like you have tested positive for Tuberculosis."

I tried to explain that I had a negative TB test before surgery and another negative test afterwards. And that I was fairly certain that I was still negative. "You know that gives us the right to come to your house. I know you have a roommate, and we want to see his passport. We want to know all about him. We are going to go through all your drawers. We are going to check everything in your home. The nurse showed up about this time, and I asked the lady to leave. On the way out the door, she replied, "I know you are being discharged on Thanksgiving Day. You need to answer your door when we get there."

It was about noon on Thanksgiving Day when I got home. I was in so much pain. I told my partner that we were leaving the next day for Florida. By 8:30 a.m. the following Monday morning my phone was ringing. "Mr. Foster, this is the Dallas County

Health Department. You need to answer this door. Otherwise, I'll have the sheriff out here," she said.

I quickly mentioned that I was not there and instructed her to leave. I then told her that she would be receiving a letter from my attorney and that certified mail addressed to her had already gone out. I never heard from her again, but I had the feeling that she was more interested in my partner than she was in me. They had already tried to find every spec of dirt they could about me, but there was none. There was none on my partner either, but they didn't know that.

Several years after the death of Barry Pelton, one of his sisters asked if I could help with getting Barry inducted into the Garland Sports Hall of Fame. She told me about how their dad had lost the family farm at Liberty Grove during the Great Depression. She also mentioned about the family moving around from place to place before spending almost ten years as sharecroppers on the famed Goforth farm near White Rock Lake. After their dad died as a result of diabetes in 1945, their mother then moved the unmarried children into a house near downtown Garland. Nine-year-old Barry was just like us kids out in the country. He grew up with an outhouse out back.

Barry's sister would complain about his being out in the yard and hitting his tennis balls against the house all day. She says it was all day, every day. As time went on, Barry and Buddy Walker became good friends, which proved to be the best of both worlds since Buddy's dad, Bud Walker, was the tennis coach. Barry and Buddy played in the evenings and on weekends. They obviously got more coaching than the other Garland High School students, and it paid off. They won state championship title for GHS two years in a row. First in 1951, then again in 1952. This put Garland on the map as far as tennis was concerned.

FROM THE OUTHOUSE TO THE COURTHOUSE

The following year, Barry and Jerry Shelton went on to win the state championship. That was the year that Barry graduated GHS. A tennis scholarship allowed him to attend East Texas State, where he received bachelor's and master's degrees. But Garland's Director of Athletics would not be kind to Barry. Homer Johnson and his pent-up bias and prejudice against Barry would finally surface in later years.

Barry died in 1987 and was nominated to the Garland Sports Hall of Fame the following year. Nothing ever happened with that nomination. His sister saw Homer in a downtown Garland restaurant about five years later and ask Homer about the nomination. She also stated that Barry's mother was approaching 100 years of age and was clinging to life so that she could live to see her youngest child receive his due honor. Homer replied, "Not to worry. We'll get there."

But they never got there. I was then asked to get involved. I called the new AD. He had been anointed by Johnson. He asked if I would submit another application, which I did. One year went by, then a second. So I called and was told that my application was still in his desk drawer. I began asking more and more questions. Those questions were never answered. But then one day, I finally got the answer that explained it all. Another area historian told me that he had also submitted an application. Five years went by without any action. Then one day he saw Homer face to face, and he decided it was time for a confrontation. "Homer, why is Barry Pelton the only GHS tennis champion not in the Sports Hall of Fame?" he asked. Homer curtly replied, "That queer SOB will never be in the Sports Hall of Fame as long as I am living."

Homer Johnson has crossed the river of life now. I am certainly not the person to pass any judgement as to who might be, or not be, greeted by St. Peter.

CHAPTER 6

# My Introduction into Politics

It was a cold day in December when the doctor, and the sisters, delivered me at the old St. Paul Hospital in downtown Dallas. This was back during World War II while my dad was home on leave. The mother and baby would typically remain in the hospital for several days back then. So, on the fourth day the doctor told my dad that he could take us home the following day. After all, it would be Christmas Day.

It was customary for the funeral homes to operate an ambulance service in those days. My dad had made arrangements with Cecil Williams the previous day to borrow his ambulance. It was cold that day and there was no heater in my dad's car. He left the funeral home and headed down Garland Road, then on past White Rock Lake before making his way over to St Paul Hospital. He had no trouble finding reserved parking for "Ambulance Only."

After my mother and I were comfortably positioned in the front seat, he headed over to the home of his parents at Liberty Grove. Several family members had already started to gather for their annual Christmas dinner. This was out in the country near the Dallas and Rockwall county line. The air was cold and crisp. Any sound would carry for a country mile. As we rounded the corner and headed up the hill, my dad pressed the siren starter button as we approached the house. That loud siren could be heard all over the countryside.

Everyone in the house ran toward the door. Neighbors for miles around jumped into their car and headed over to the J. A. Foster homeplace. They soon discovered that no one had been seriously injured. But a new grandson by the name of Jimmy had arrived. My grandmother never got over that. The sound of a siren frightened her the rest of her life.

After my tour of duty in the U.S. Army and during the latter days of my tenure with Johnson & Johnson, I began to get involved in Dallas County politics. At that time, I truly thought I could make a difference. I even believed that I could help bring qualified candidates into office. I believed that they would serve their fellow constituents in a professional and dignified manner. I was wrong.

My first candidate screening panel assignment set me back several weeks. It was sometime around 1978. We were meeting in the basement of the Warren Avenue Methodist Church. The very first candidates to appear before the committee were none other than John Wiley Price and Charles Rose. We were all neatly positioned in our chairs lined up behind a row of folding tables. Price got the first question and then it went to Rose. Rose accused Price of some impropriety. Then Price, in a fit of rage, threw a strong right hook and knocked Rose to the floor. Rose got up with blood squirting from both nostrils.

Members of the screening committee jumped up and attempted to push their chairs back, only to discover they were up against the wall. Both were told to leave. The committee members then took a break in order to regain our composure. My political drive was suddenly diminished. Charles Rose later served as justice of the peace in Dallas County for several years. John Wiley Price was elected Dallas County Commissioner in 1985 and is still serving as of 2022.

Sometime around 1995, my grandmother was visiting and I took her to my office over in Oak Cliff near what would become known as the Bishop Arts District. I gave her a tour of my alarm business office and about halfway through the tour, she paused. She looked at me and said, "You know when you were a small child, Dr. Brooks had to come to the house to check on you. You were suffering from asthma. As he was leaving, he stopped, looked at me, and said, 'I'm not sure he will make it to adulthood.' I wish he could see you know." Then I remarked that I would be sheriff one day. She replied, "I'm sure you will."

As we entered 2003, I decided that it was time to make an attempt at fulfilling that promise. It would be an understatement to say that I was politically naive. Unfortunately, I grew up trusting people. I thought folks were honest. It didn't take long to learn otherwise, though. I soon discovered that it would be a long, bumpy road ahead. Several friends were already telling me that Dallas County commissioners had decided that it was time for Sheriff Jim Bowles to go. But there was a fly in the ointment. Commissioners wanted their guy on the inside. They wanted someone that would listen to them and do things their way.

There is no question that Bowles had recently received a ton of bad press. Most had been over a $20 million jail commissary contract with his friend Jack Madera. According to the *Morning News,* Madera's company, Mid-America Services, had an expense account set up for the sheriff. He was getting travel expenses, in addition to meal expenses. Madera's company had also agreed to turn over $600,000 to the sheriff's department annually. Two other venders were offering to turn over more than $1.2 million each year. This was a serious chunk of change. It was widely rumored that a certain alpha male commissioner wanted access to those transactions.

An elaborate scheme was put into play. A high-level deputy was handpicked to run against Bowles. But everyone knew that Bowles would fire the deputy once he discovered that his name had been thrown into the hat. This scheme would work only if their man was transferred to another department. He needed to be protected. Danny Chandler was handpicked for this position. A new department and a new position was created. Chandler was transferred. He would now report to the county judge. He could now safely run against the incumbent sheriff.

I'm not aware that Chandler accomplished much in the way of homeland security during this time. But he was on the county payroll and would have no problem defeating Bowles. But the victory would be short lived. There was a storm brewing. And it was over on the Democratic side of the ticket. It seems that I got into the race early on. Campaign records indicate that I filed for the office of Dallas County Sheriff on December 4, 2003. Soon afterwards, I set up a large campaign headquarters on Lancaster Avenue. According to a February 26, 2004, article in the *White Rocker*, it appears that I was still the only candidate.

Being the sole candidate felt good. But that feeling was temporary. Other candidates began to jump into the race. Charles Munoz and Lupe Valdez soon made it a three-way contest. Of course, I had a significant lead. Munoz and Valdez were a little late getting out of the gate. Their campaigns were lagging behind. Then Sam Allen, a fourth candidate, appeared on the scene. Sam knew how to impress the voters. He was a large-framed African-

American man that very much enjoyed parading around the various early voting locations. He always wore his wide-brimmed cowboy hat as he smiled and greeted voters. Then he would hand each and every one an oversized, glossy business card complete with a photo of him in that white cowboy hat.

Campaigning was over for Chandler. He had defeated Bowles with a 17,000-vote lead. But the Democrats would spend all day, every day for the next two weeks at early voting locations. I had picked the Beckley Sub-courthouse in Oak Cliff, since it had previously been the number one voter turnout location. On the fourth day of early voting, I began to focus my attention on a Dallas maintenance worker. He had been showing up every day at the same time. Always in the same Dallas County vehicle and always with a large laptop computer. He always went straight to the electronic polling equipment and after a while would return to his vehicle and leave.

This routine was repeated about three times every day. I wasted no time asking one of the county employees about our "mystery man" and was told that he was assigned to the maintenance department which reports to none other than Commissioner Price. I needed to speak to the person in charge of this early voting location. Since candidates are not allowed inside the polls, I waited until the doors were locked and she was leaving.

It was already getting dark. I walked up to her car just as she unlocked the door. She recognized me and didn't seem alarmed. I then asked, "Mavis, why is this man coming in with a laptop computer several times each day and connecting it to your voting equipment?"

Mavis responded, "Oh he works for the county. He is calibrating the voting equipment." When I ask if she had called him out, the response was no. I responded. "You know that you are in charge.

You are the only person with authority to call someone out and work on the equipment." To which she replied, "You need to talk with Senator West about that." This was my first clue that West and Price were like glue.

She quickly closed the door on that old blue Buick sedan and headed out down Beckley Avenue. Her taillights were soon out of sight. I never did know exactly what he was doing or why he was there. I'm not sure what might have been accomplished by our conversation, but it was the last time that I saw the "calibration man" running around with his computer. The last time I checked, he was still employed by the county.

Once the Democratic votes were tallied, Munoz and Allen were out of the race. There would be a runoff election. Foster and Valdez would be the only two names appearing on the entire ballot. My thoughts turned to how do we get folks out to vote for a runoff. But they should have been directed to all the activity taking place behind the scenes.

I soon began seeing Valdez for Sheriff signs everywhere. They were even on the back of DART buses. It seemed as if every other bus had one of her signs across its rear end. I began to ask questions. I wanted to know where she was getting all that money. The answer came fairly soon. But I initially thought it couldn't be true. Several friends with ties to the party headquarters had told me that the chair was using party funds to support Valdez. I suppose that might be legal, but she bankrupted the Dallas County Democratic Party in the process. The new party chair would have to take out a loan the following year just to pay matching payroll taxes.

Needless to say, with that kind of financial support Valdez won the runoff. But I suppose it was a blessing in disguise. Price wanted to control the sheriff, and I would not have been happy with that. I also doubt that I would have been in a position to call for a federal investigation of JWP. Nor would I have been in a position to call for an investigation of other elected officials. Yes, they were all Democrats. And it was soon known that I was not the darling of the Democratic Party, but I felt that I had to clean up the corruption, regardless of party affiliation.

Traveling down the path of standing up for what is right and just can be a lonely road. I will never forget meeting the party chair, Darlene Ewing, in the parking lot of Dallas County Commissioners Court. This would have been after I was serving as Dallas County Judge. She seemed to be in a mad rush as she approached me. I calmly said, "You know he is going to be indicted." She then curtly turned and said, "I don't have time to talk with you." She promptly headed inside and down the hallway. I followed a short distance behind. Then I noticed that JWP was anxiously waiting for her. He quickly closed the door once she was inside.

I often wondered if she remained loyal after his indictment. The news media seemed to change their minds about my ability to get things done once the DOJ held their press conference and revealed a lengthy list of indictments.

Some of my most extreme critics suddenly started warming up. They now wanted details about all the various charges. They even wanted to know the extent of his involvement with Ross Perot, Jr. After all, JWP had been recently quoted in the news as saying, "I really don't know Ross Jr. socially. I only recall meeting him once." The truth though was, Price, and Valdez, and I were on a trip to meet with the state jail commission in Austin when one of the Tarrant County commissioners asked Price if he could get him in contact with Ross Jr. Price quickly pulled a phone from his pocket and stated, "Here. Hold on just a minute. I've got him on speed dial."

CHAPTER 7

# Gearing Up for the Big One

It was back in 2006 that the Dallas County Elections Administrator, Bruce Sherbet, was speaking at a Richardson, Texas, event about the state of politics in Dallas County. I was comfortably positioned in the front row. About halfway through his presentation, Sherbet clearly mentioned that the pendulum was swinging toward the Democrats in Dallas County. It was at that moment that I could clearly see my opportunity to get back into the race. The next morning, I searched for positions that would be on the ballot.

I, along with everyone else that I knew, had a great respect for Sherbet. He was the ideal elections administrator. He had been only 19 when he got his start with the county. Four years later, he was in charge of voter registration. No one ever had a negative comment about him as elections administrator, and he had served in that position as long as I can remember.

Price had been one of his most ardent supporters for years. He even bought a dress for Bruce's first daughter when she was born in 1989. But suddenly, the tables were turned. It appeared that my successor, Clay Jenkins, was asking for Sherbet's resignation. I seriously doubt that was the case, though, especially since a meeting of the elections commission had been called. The purpose of that commission would be to appoint a new elections administrator. Jenkins would not have enough political experience or savvy to know about the commission. Only one person would be driving that bus. It would be none other than John Wiley Price.

Sherbet went to Price, thinking that one of his loyal supporters could turn this ship around. Price looked Sherbet square in the eye and said, "I think it's time for you to move on." Sherbet later explained that no reason was ever given. The truth is that JWP wanted to be in control of all Dallas County government. In reality, he was already in charge of most every aspect of it. One by one, over the years he had quietly managed to gain control of most every department. It didn't matter if it was juvenile justice, security, or the maintenance department. Price wanted complete control. He also wanted control of the boards and commissions. I will never forget a wise man telling me years earlier, "Beware of a banker who never take a holiday." And he was right. Price didn't even want to take a day off for his mother's funeral. He told one of the reporters that he thought his mother would want him to be on the job and taking care of his responsibilities instead of attending her funeral.

Price had handpicked Toni Pippins-Poole to replace Sherbet. She remained on the job for eight years before a scandal finally broke. It was reported that 9,000 election ballots were never turned in. It also seems that $6 million had been spent the previous year on election equipment that couldn't be used. The county couldn't even properly store the equipment. One of my chief complaints during my term as county judge was that election equipment is stored in a warehouse under the control of JWP.

This complaint never seemed to get traction. I went over to that warehouse. Anyone could just walk in at any time. That equipment needed to be under lock and key. But apparently this is the way Price wanted it.

After Sherbet left, he said, "John broke my heart. I loved and respected him. At one time he was a person of principles." Collin County, Texas, was fortunate to get Sherbet as their county elections administrator in 2015.

Experience from my previous campaign helped guide me as I entered the race for county judge. I wanted an under-the-radar campaign. I believed that a high-profile race would draw unwanted attention. The incumbent Margaret Kelliher did just the opposite. She had her photo posted on billboards all across Dallas and the outlying areas. I was criticized for waiting until the last minute to file. The truth was that I had been told that state senator David Cain was going to enter the race. I knew it would be a waste of my time and resources if he were a candidate. I privately turned in my fee and other required documents to the party chair. I told her that I would be standing by, but if Cain filed, then I would withdraw. He never appeared, and my intent to run was made official.

I attended almost every event possible handing out my trifold brochure. I even attended a historical gathering late one afternoon in Grand Prairie before hopping over to Oak Lawn for the dedication of their memorial statue. Before the campaign was over, I had placed more than 11,000 brochures into the hands of our voters, not to mention all the doors that I knocked on.

Margaret Kelliher was from Highland Park. She had a large campaign war chest. Several influential friends suggested that I not run against her, but I did. Democratic commissioner Price posed for a photo with Kelliher and a few other Republicans.

He even mailed out a giant photo of the group with printed instruction that mentioned them by name. It concluded with "Then Push The D Button At The Ballot Box." They all thought he was doing them a huge favor. It was even reported that they gladly made significant contributions to his campaign. The truth of the matter is that I overheard him bragging about this one day. He was telling another commissioner, "They didn't realize that if you hit the D button, that all other votes are cancelled."

Photo from Price campaign mailer: "I am asking you to vote the Democratic Lever. However, the people pictured are good people, doing a great job. I ask you to vote them on our team." Left to right: Judge David Evans, Margaret Kelliher, Lisa Hembry, John Wiley Price, Judge Ada Brown and Judge Manny Alvarez.

In reality, Price knew that as soon as you pressed the Democratic button, all the other votes were cancelled. I mistakenly thought they were his friends.

On election night, all the Republicans had gathered for their watch party, and I was with all the Democrats. It was early on when a friend called me from the Republican gathering. He reported that there was some tension building. It was even thought that I would likely defeat the incumbent. The race moved back and forth all through the evening. A large crowd had gathered early on, but by 10:00 p.m. the crowd began to thin.

It was now becoming crystal-clear. Many Democrats would be swept into office that night. We would have a new county judge, district attorney, county treasurer, district clerk and other district judges. And no, I did not receive a call from the incumbent that night. She even made it clear that she didn't want to speak to me and that I was not especially welcome at any meeting of the commissioner's court.

I complied with those wishes, but in hindsight, I believe that it would have been beneficial to attend several meetings. The next night, my partner and I were out for a quiet dinner when Kevin Krause with the *Dallas Morning News* called. His first words were "Judge Foster, it looks like I am going to be required to put the part about you being gay in the news tomorrow morning." I asked, "Why would you want to do that?" He responded, "It's not me. They are making me do it."

It was soon revealed that my predecessor was a close friend of the editor of the *News.* My theory was that she thought the negative press would somehow do me in. Frances James, the Cemetery Lady, was the only person that commented on the matter. A day or two later Frances, looked over at me and quietly said, "I don't know why they thought it necessary to put that part in the newspaper about you being gay."

Then on January 1, 2007, my predecessor was gone. We had the distinct honor of being sworn into office by the legendary Judge Barefoot Sanders (forced Dallas Schools to integrate). The next day I was in the office, and we were holding court. It looked to me like every news station and every newspaper reporter in North Texas was present that day. My routine duties soon included listening to complaints about wrongdoing by public and elected officials. Those complaints included voter fraud, abuse of office, and a wide range of other improprieties.

My secretary walked into the office one day and quietly told me that Linda Wilson didn't have an appointment but wanted to speak to me. I asked her to show the lady in. We sat at the conference table, and she wasted no time in telling me about a deputy constable that came to her apartment and offered to make her traffic tickets disappear in exchange for sexual favors. I promptly stood up and told the lady to wait just a moment. I then stepped out and asked the secretary to please find Peggy Lundy, my executive assistant, and court administrator Daryl Martin. I needed them to stop whatever they were doing and come to my office immediately.

Both Lundy and Martin arrived within a minute or two. Once they were seated, I asked Wilson if she would fill us in on the details. Wilson then explained, "My troubles all started after I got to the Beckley Courthouse. They told me the constables were located upstairs. When I got up there, they sent me to see Lt. Howard Watson. I ask him if he could help me. I told him that I got a ticket and couldn't pay it and that a warrant had been issued for my arrest. He gave me a card with his name and phone number on it. I got his card right here. He told me to call the next day. He needed time to work on it. So, I called back the next day and that's when my troubles all really started."

After a brief pause, I asked Wilson if she could tell us what happened the next day. Wilson then said, "I sure can. Lieutenant Watson told me he needed more time to check on it. He said he would call me back. The next day he called me and said he needed to come by my place. He had some papers for me. When he got there, he mentioned that he left the papers in the trunk of his car and then he wanted to see my bedroom. Then he wanted to get into bed with me. So I let him. Before he left, he told me that he was still working on the warrant. He called me a few days later and wanted to come back. It was the same story again, but this time a friend of mine showed up just as he was leaving. When I told her what was going on, she told me that I got to let somebody know what is happening. So, that is why I am here."

I asked the court administrator to make sure that her information got over to the DA's office so that Watson could be prosecuted. As it turned out, Constable Cortes had hired Watson without even conducting a background check. Watson had a very checkered background, and most agencies would have never hired him. I have often wondered if Cortes knew about his employment history and hired him anyway. One of the TV news reporters had already received a tip about Watson and the reporter's camera operator was secretly videotaping Watson as he used his personal "police-looking car" on frequent traffic stops. The traffic stops were usually near the Beckley Courthouse, and the driver was almost always a younger woman. Watson would then question them for a few minutes before he sent them on their way.

Watson didn't even meet Dallas County minimum requirements for being a deputy constable. He had previously worked as a private detective and briefly worked for two small town police departments with a total combined experience of six months. It was later reported that Watson's wife was a cousin of chief deputy Ken Hines. Watson was soon promoted to sergeant even though he couldn't pass a background check. Even though unqualified, he was later promoted to lieutenant.

Watson would soon face indictment on a wide array of charges. He had bought a 2000 Ford Crown Victoria and then refused to pay for the balance of the purchase price. He even threatened the seller with a gun. Watson promptly outfitted the Crown Vic with siren, police emergency light and radio. There was one problem, though. He couldn't get title to the automobile. He was unable to get permanent tags, so he used his connection at the county tax office, located on the first floor of the Beckley Courthouse. He was down there every month renewing his paper tags, which opened the door to another investigation.

Ex-Lieutenant Watson was convicted on August 8, 2011, for unauthorized use of a motor vehicle. It would be the first indictment stemming from the constable's investigation, which Price adamantly opposed. Other convictions would soon follow. Watson pled guilty on September 23, 2011, to two felony charges of bribery and two counts of sexual assault. He was sentenced to one year in state jail and 10 years probation. He was also required to register as a sex offender. The DA's office reportedly offered him a lighter sentence in exchange for information and testimony that would be used in another investigation.

Original bail was set at $173,000 dollars but was increased to $281,000 a few days later. Then for some unexplained reason it was reduced to $71,000. Watson posted bail and was allowed to remove his ankle monitor and move out of town. He relocated to Mount Pleasant, Texas. His wife, Janette, was also arrested on charges pertaining to the alteration of a vehicle title and providing false information.

Commissioners Court had hired Danny Defenbaugh, former FBI Special Agent in Charge, to conduct an investigation of two constables and their practice of towing vehicles. Those vehicles were driven predominately by undocumented residents. The majority of those vehicles were never claimed, and the towing company had accumulated thousands of vehicles. It is difficult to imagine that so many vehicles could be towed by one company. One estimate had the total at close to 13,000. One news reporter put it this way. "Two elected officials and one private company are preying on those that can least afford it. They are the innocent victims." Investigations of other officials would follow.

CHAPTER 8

# The Big Shakedown

One of the first complaints I had was about the bail bond board. Price was not the chair of that board, but every item on the agenda required his approval if it was to pass. I had already been asked if I thought JWP was getting a kickback from some of the bail bond companies. I ask the complainant why he thought that. He calmly replied, "Well, I have checked the license plate number on several of his vintage cars. Almost everyone comes back to a person that is in, or was in, prison. I am thinking they put those automobiles up for collateral on their bond. Then at a certain time of the day, I almost always see his car parked out in front of Delta Bail Bond Company."

As previously mentioned, Price was not chairman of the bail bond board, but he ruled it with an iron fist. According to one news reporter, "He was a master at taking campaign contributions and finding ways to transfer those donations into cash in such a way that it would appear as a legitimate expense. Those funds would then be placed directly into the pockets of JWP. He even found time on most Sundays to shop for art. African art piqued his interest. He would stop by a Dallas gallery operated by Karen Manning. He like to walk in and view the art prior to making his "purchase" with a check from his campaign account. Ms. Manning would typically keep $45 of the "purchase" and the rest of the cash was then handed over to Price. The FBI reports that Manning transferred more than $100,000 to Price from June 2004 through May 2010.

Dallas County exercised little oversight over the bond companies. A report in 2011 indicated that bondspersons owed Dallas County $35 million in forfeited bonds, and no one seemed to even know it. Or maybe the guy that controlled the board was deliberately looking in the other direction. Bond forfeiture money is intended to go into the county treasury. In Dallas it almost always is left in the hands of bond companies. There is usually no hearing, and if one is held, there is almost never a record of that hearing.

Any potential kickback from a bail bond company concerned me, but little did I know that the granddaddy of all kickback schemes was yet to come. It was on April 13, 2007, that I attended the grand opening for a large logistics project. It was known as the Dallas Logistics Hub and was the largest logistics park under development in North America. The master plan included 6,000 acres with 60 million square feet of distribution, manufacturing, and office and retail space.

This huge event was sponsored by the Allen Group (TAG). I soon discovered that other elected officials were in attendance. Texas Secretary of State Roger Williams and U.S. Representative Eddie Bernice Johnson were among the many mayors and others in attendance. One of the officials introduced me, along with one of the Dallas County Commissioners, to Richard Allen. It was explained that the group had already built rail and truck yards in south Dallas. These yards were twice as big as those servicing Perot's Alliance Airport in Fort Worth.

Allen extended a cordial welcome and explained that he could really use my help. He then mentioned that he would arrange a meeting in a few days. The decision was made to hold the meeting at the office of attorney John H. Barr, instead of my office. It was at that meeting he revealed how Price had attempted to block his project. My initial reaction was shock and disbelief, but I then reflected back on the various other complaints as reality began to suddenly set in. I quickly realized that Price had indeed played a key role in an attempt to block this project, a project that he should have been solidly behind. The project would bring thousands of jobs to southern Dallas County and would bring unprecedented growth to JWP's district.

It wasn't long before I discovered that Representative Johnson had already confronted Price about his attempt to block this project. She had been one of the first to be contacted by Allen. Price was not pleased with her attempt to intervene. He then explained that a group known as SALT (Service and Leadership Team) had been formed to make certain that men of southern Dallas got a cut of that project. The SALT group, all friends of Price, consisted of former Dallas Cowboys football player Pettis Norman, radio personality Willis Johnson, Commissioner John Wiley Price, and former Citibank loan officer John Edmonds. The group claimed to want equity in the project.

The congresswoman had called a meeting between Allen and the SALT group in an effort to smooth things over. Pettis Norman and the group made it clear that they were very unhappy that Allen had complained to the Rep. Johnson. Price claims to have attended the meeting, and he was also highly agitated, according to a Dallas Observer reporter Jim Schutze. Price later returned to her office with State Senator Royce West. JWP told her that the three of them together were the toughest elected officials in southern Dallas County and that if they stuck together, they could get a lot of things done. He then added, "Allen and his group is not going to come in here and there not be some black folks making money. They really need to leave some money here in the black community."

Johnson was first contacted by Allen in 2005, and here we were in 2007 with the problem continuing to worsen. Price had even added an addendum to the court docket that would add property belonging to Ross Perot, Jr., to the original court order. I knew that the initial proposal had already been approved by the Dallas Fort Worth Airport Board and that any change to the original plan would delay the project. The project, in its entirety, would require approval by a board that met only once a month. And there was no assurance that it would pass, especially since members represent outlying counties such as Collin, Denton, and Tarrant (Fort Worth).

I considered this a delay tactic. Commissioners Dickey and Mayfield, along with myself, opposed the change. The addendum failed. Price was furious. He drew his fist back as if he intended to hit me. I had to adjourn court until he calmed down. Several days later, I received a call from State Senator Royce West. This was at 5:00 p.m. on a Friday, and he wanted to know if I would stop by his office. I agreed and headed in that direction.

As soon as I walked in the door there was John Wiley Price standing in the lobby waiting for me. It was apparent where we were headed. West, in his reverberating voice, said, "Now Foster, you need to get with us on this hub project. You need to get over with the Democrats." I explained that my mind was made up and it would not change. That's when West began banging his fist on his oak desk with each and every word. "Damn it. We need to get control of that inland port," he shouted.

After a few more unpleasant exchanges, I excused myself and headed home. A few minutes later, my cell phone was ringing, and it was Mayor Tom Leppert. He said, "Judge Foster, this is Mayor Leppert. You are on the prevailing side, so you can place the order about the inland port back on the agenda. Can I count on you to do that?" he asked. I explained that I would give it some serious thought over the weekend.

That next Tuesday morning Senator West was standing in front of my office. A court order had already been prepared, and he wanted me to place it on the agenda. I explained that it was not going to happen. Neither he nor Price was happy. I could see JWP wanting to line his pockets, but I gave the mayor more credit. After all, a project like this would have been the best thing that could have happened to the southern sector of Dallas County. Five years into the project, Leppert and Price threw their weight behind an eighteen month "Land Use" study for the project. Allen already had commitments from companies such as Whirlpool and others. An eighteen-month delay soon began to bring a slow death to what would have become an economic hub for the southern sector.

Jim Schutze with the *Dallas Observer* had interviewed Representative Johnson in December of 2008. During that interview, he quoted her as saying, "I see all of these different deals that John's trying to do over the years, shaking people down and all that kind of stuff." Schultze also interviewed me on the same subject. He asked if I thought Price had been involved in a shakedown. My response was "Some say that he is involved in a shakedown." JWP then sued Johnson and also sued me.

He soon found out that suing the congresswoman was not going to work. He also found out during my deposition that he was under federal investigation. That's when life, as he knew it, began to change.

In looking back, I had a few conversations with Richard Allen. He never admitted it, but Johnson always felt that JWP killed what would have been the largest logistic park in North America. Richard Allen could have just forked over the $500,000 annually, but he was a man of principal. He lost a fortune, but he stood up for what he believed in.

Price may have mistakenly believed that he had gotten away with his role in their carefully orchestrated charade. But eventually he was held accountable. During his corruption trial, an official with the company owned by the Perot family was called to testify. He stated that in 2007 money was being funneled to a female associate of Price. A news article later reported that the purpose of that money was to kill the Inland Port, also known as Dallas Logistics Center. A witness also testified that the Dallas Logistics Hub would have been in direct competition with the Perot family's air and rail freight center in Fort Worth.

The Perot family was not a defendant in the trial. The government made it perfectly clear that no wrongdoing by the Perot family was found. Its testimony did shed light on the subject, though. That female associate of Price was later revealed to be Kathy Nealy. She was the direct link to the money from Perot to Price. But she couldn't be prosecuted, since the government granted her immunity during the Don Hill (Dallas City Council) trial and that immunity had never been revoked.

Nealy had her share of problems with the federal government. One of those looming problems stemmed from a 2006 IRS levy registered with the Dallas County Tax Appraiser against her condo. By 2011 the IRS claimed that she owed $459,000 in federal taxes, interest, and penalties.

June 27, 2011, would be a new day in Dallas. The voters had clearly spoken. Their new mayor would be Mike Rawlings. Nealy had earned close to $305,000 for her role in mustering the voters in the southern sector and now Rawlins, Nealy and a list of other campaign workers were about to glory in the spotlight.

The much-anticipated inauguration was about to take place. Rawlings was due to make his speech and be sworn in just a few minutes. He, along with city officials, county officials, mayors from surrounding cities and an entire host of news reporters were present at a city hall for the big event. It was a standing-room-only crowd.

Speakers were at the podium as the audience quietly listened to the preliminary remarks being made. Rawlins had stepped up to the microphone just as text messages began to ring out all through the crowd. Officials began to quietly exit with their cellphones still in their hand. Rawlings instinctively knew that a serious problem had developed, but he had no clue as to what it might be.

News reporters also sensed there was a bigger fish to fry and began following those making a mad dash toward their cars. They didn't have far to go. It was precisely 9:00 a.m. on this day that FBI and IRS agents simultaneously executed search warrants on the homes and offices of Kathy Nealy, John Wiley Price, and his assistant Dapheny Fain.

Attorneys representing Nealy asked for, and received, special permission to have her removed from the trial. Her attorneys claim that federal prosecutors granted her immunity during the Don Hill trial and that her immunity was never rescinded. Federal Judge Barbara Lynn granted her request. It was thought that Nealy would stand trial later, but she never did.

Price stood helplessly by as agents loaded box after box of evidence from his office. He even complained about the inconvenience they were causing. One of the agents, not sure if it was Don Sherman or not, wasn't impressed. He looked at Price and said, "This is the first day of the rest of your life." They also simultaneously appeared at his Oak Cliff home. A locksmith was called in so that a large safe could be unlocked. Once opened, there it was. $220,000 in crisp $100 bills. They were all lined up and neatly arranged in a row. There was also a collection of expensive watches in addition to other items. Now, just so everyone knows, anything of value in that safe was seized as evidence.

It was reported that his loyal assistant, Dapheny Fain, had one room in her home set up as a shrine to JWP. She was also storing his big, shiny, black Bentley in her garage. There is no question that Price was fascinated with both expensive and vintage cars. It is interesting though that at least six of his thirteen vintage cars required a special hearing in order to clear up their titles. That process requires a special administrative hearing and a ruling from the Dallas County Tax Office. Price knew the process well. He had been there more than once.

It was noted earlier in this book in the section about bail bonds that the majority of Price's vintage cars came from men that were in prison. The Bentley would be no exception. You may recall the big scandal at Baylor Hospital. It was the one where an employee was withdrawing funds electronically. Her son, Gary Stephens, was the beneficiary. He went on a year-long spending spree buying speed boats, luxury cars, and anything else that he wanted. A year later he had tired of it.

He had purchased the Bentley in New York. Price soon found

it at Andretti Motors in Oak Lawn. But Andretti didn't have clear title to the vehicle. He needed Stephens to return and sign some documents. Neither did he have access to Stephens. He was already in jail over in Tarrant County. Shady deals were like a magnet. They always seemed to attract John Wiley Price. And here is where Danny Faulkner enters the picture. Those of you that were around in the late 1970s will remember the savings and loan scandal. It hit the Dallas area hardest but made national news.

Faulkner had served four of his twenty-year sentence before he was released after being diagnosed with cancer. The doctor claimed that he had six months to live. But they were wrong. It would be another thirteen years before his death. He and Price were not strangers. JWP referred to him as Uncle Danny. He and a few others had served on Price's original campaign team. Their history goes beyond that though. If we go back a little farther, we will find that Price almost served time in the federal penitentiary. His political career was almost derailed before he was able to get it off the ground.

It was back around 1975 when a Dallas bank filed charges against him. It claimed that he made a false statement on a loan application. Price was ready to plead guilty, but the judge refused to sign off on the plea. A trial date was then set. Price was found guilty and sentenced to six months in jail. He appealed the sentence on the grounds that his attorney was totally unprepared to defend him, and the verdict was overturned.

I have wondered for years if Faulkner suggested or was involved in the $100,000 loan Price received from the First National Bank in Garland. This would have been prior to its being closed by federal regulators. I do see where Price took out a loan for $53,000 just prior to Faulkner's being indicted. He frequently asked for, and was granted, an extension. He even returned and took out another loan for close to $140,000. Shortly afterwards, the FDIC closed the bank and sued Price. He agreed to pay $150,00 in order to resolve the case.

One of the attorneys representing Price was quoted in a news article as he attempted to justify the purchase of the Bentley. He claimed that Price was trading up. He had traded a Dodge Viper and then a 2003 BMW as he made his way up to more expensive automobiles. That attorney failed to mention, though, where the Dodge Viper came from. The original seller was none other than Danny Faulkner.

Faulkner had previously sold about nine acres of land out on Grady Niblo Road to Wayne White. Price wanted that land. Every Sunday afternoon he would show up at White's antique shop in Mesquite, which was rented from Faulkner. Price pretended to be interested in playing dominoes. But White could see through the smoke. He realized that JWP really wanted to get his hands on that land.

As time went on, he agreed to sell. That was until he discovered that Price wanted the title in Jack Madera's name. Madera had a jail commissary contract with Jim Bowles. "My," said the spider, "what a fine web you weave." All of White's friends advised him to stay clear of Jack Madera, so he refused. But he later agreed to proceed with the sale. But it looked as if the property would have a "clouded title."

In case you are wondering how I know about all of this, remember that the FBI would ask me questions from time to time. Also, remember that I grew up in Rowlett, and Faulkner's home base was operating in that town. My sister, Charlotte, even showed up one Christmas Day in a Rolls Royce. When I ask her to explain the Rolls, she quickly mentioned that Danny was flying around in the helicopter and let them borrow his car.

The reason that the subject even came to light was that Price was selling the property. Federal agents were concerned but felt there was little that could be done to prevent the sale. They had already checked the history. They thought it was strange that JWP bought the land twice in one day. Once from White and once from his assistant, Dapheny Fain. They checked a little deeper and discovered Faulkner had been ordered by the court to sell the property and turn the receipts over to the government. That's how Price became the proud owner of what would later become prime property.

Suddenly, all the dots were connected. Republic Title in Dallas was handling the transaction. Federal agents showed up early on the day of closing. They wasted no time asking if they had a check in the amount of $550,000 for John Wiley Price. The answer was crystal clear: "Yes, we do." One agent replied, "OK, here is a court order. Mark the check VOID. Make another check for the exact same amount. Make it payable to the U.S. Marshals Service. Then let me have that check. We will wait right here while you do that. This is your copy of the court order," the agent said.

Billy Ravkind had successfully convinced the court to pay all attorney fees for Price. Little did Price know that the court would claim any and all cash that they could get their hands on. That included the $220,000 in crisp $100 bills found inside his safe. It also included the $550,000 proceeds for the sale of the Grady Niblo property.

I will never forget a favorite expression of one of the veteran Dallas police officers. The officer would often say, "He can beat the rap, but he can't beat the ride." It has been conservatively estimated that the ride cost Price close to $1.2 million, not to mention his reputation. And his playmates suddenly lost interest in playing ball with the former alpha male.

CHAPTER 9

# The Lost Son

Laura Miller was our former Dallas mayor and also a former writer for *D Magazine.* She had a way with words. Her lengthy 1991 article in that magazine really summed up the life of John Wiley Price—at least his life as she saw it at that time. She called him "The Hustler." While it may be difficult to imagine, Dave Fox, the founder of the Fox and Jacobs construction firm and a former Dallas County Judge, thought that he could mentor Price. He actually believed that there was potential there. He took Price in and treated him like a son. He later regretted ever knowing Price.

It was a cold morning in late February when Miller interviewed Fox. The interview took place in a conference room overlooking downtown Dallas. It was a fitting backdrop, since this was the city that Fox had helped build. He told Miller that at one time he held out big hopes for Price. Then he went on to say, "But that was before Price became a rebel. I treated him like a son. Wanted him to become the first black mayor of Dallas. Now he is ready to turn against me. He will turn against me, or anyone else that gets in his way. He's ready to sacrifice our friendship for his radical injustice."

Photo source, *Dallas Morning News*, 1990.

An army of news reporters follows Price as he leaves Crimes Against Persons Department at Dallas Police Headquarters after turning over the gun used in the Bernal altercation.

Fox then went on with additional details. He slowly shook his head as if he regretted his involvement. "I wanted him to be successful in business. A leader. A coalition builder. I wanted him to be a man that could pull this city together. And he could have," Fox said. Price had already announced plans to run for congress the following year. Fox says that he wanted him to remain in Dallas and not be off in Washington, D.C. In hindsight we can now see why Price was so hostile to Congresswoman Eddie Bernice Johnson.

Price had been placed on probation the previous year after staging a publicity stunt. He had managed to climb up on the platform of one of the freeway billboards. Just as the news media arrived, JWP started painting over a large advertisement that he claimed targeted minority cigarette or beer users. Price was arrested and placed on probation. Several months later, he was out in front of his Oak Cliff home when Robert Bernal, an off-duty Dallas police officer, jogged by. He claims that Bernal shouted an insult toward him. Price took off in pursuit and a scuffle ensued. The entire incident caused several near riots in Dallas.

Bernal admitted that he had shouted an insult at Price. But according to the police report, Price pointed an Uzi submachine gun at the off-duty officer. Several prosecutors wanted to revoke his probation. They felt Price should be in jail. The officer was placed on desk duty and scheduled for additional training. But tensions across Dallas would continue to build. And Fox claims that Price was the main force driving those tensions.

An article in the *Chicago Sun Times* mentions that Price had issued a "call to arms." Police Chief Mack Vines had recently authorized an affirmative action policy and soon received praise from leaders in the minority community. Vines was then fired. Price, and others, claimed that they would take to the streets if Vines was replaced with one of the "good ole boys." In a statement to the media, Price warned, "There will be a call to arms. We will be in the streets, M-16s and all. We will be physically shooting people. I'm serious. We are not going to tolerate it." He also advocated physical violence against the police.

Fox was devastated. He felt as if he had really never known Price. He went on to say, "I would have helped him in any way that I could. But that was before his publicity stunt with the billboards. Before he threatened to take to the streets with guns. It was before the Bernal altercation. My opinion of Price has changed. If he came to me today asking for help, I'm not sure that I would be willing to get involved. He's not the same person that I thought I knew. The person that I thought I knew was an intelligent person. He was polished. Now he acts like a complete stranger."

Miller went on to mention that Dave Fox may have known Price in his earlier life but feels Price has changed. Then she reported, "The rest of Dallas sees Price as the voice that screams at them from their TV every night, the one that is prepared to declare war on Dallas at a moment's notice. Most believe that he is a rabble-rouser. Most want to know how he can afford an $80,000 automobile on a commissioner's salary." This was not her first time to write about Price.

Fox did also mention that Price and his business partner, Larry Smith, were leasing an Exxon station off I-35 in Oak Cliff. Price had complained that NCNB Bank turned him down for a $50,000 business loan. He went on to mention that he could borrow $80,000 for a Ferrari but couldn't borrow a dime to start a business. Fox admitted that he made a personal loan to Price so that he could start his business. He wasn't comfortable offering any specifics though. He did say that the loan was being repaid—not always on time, but it was being repaid.

Miller had previously written extensively about Price and his brutal treatment of women. She revealed that Price grew up in Forney, Texas. He was the son of a part-time preacher. He met a woman after moving to Dallas. He was 19 and she was 23. Price seemed to be all about rights for the black community, but he was in a relationship with an Anglo woman. Nine months later, his father married them on Valentine's Day 1970 in a little country church near Forney.

John and Vivian had a son, but three years into their marriage they were separating. Price refused to get a divorce. It would be eight years later before he would agree to the divorce. He also refused to pay child support. He claimed that he would pay their son, John Jr., $15 if he mowed the yard but refused to pay child support. The state AG garnished his paycheck for $2,650 in 1987 and again in 1988. His ex-wife said she was disappointed about his failure to pay child support. She never understood why it was never reported in the news media.

Miller believed that it was kept out of the news because Price was close friends with Lawrence Young. Young was an African-American reporter for the *Dallas Morning News*. He and Price were close. He would even stop by the commissioner's office for frequent visits. It wasn't long before he was dating one of Price's secretaries by the name of Cora Lewis. Ms. Lewis abruptly broke off the relationship once she discovered that Young was married. He complained, and Price called her into his office and savagely reprimanded her. Ms. Lewis later claimed that Price kept after her. He claimed that her obstinance was threatening his good relationship with the press. She held her ground. Two weeks later, she was fired.

Vivian later reported that once John Jr. turned 16, his father suddenly decided that their son should live with him. He claimed that he was going hire a private tutor for John, Jr. He wanted his son to improve his grades in school. He even claimed that he wanted their son to follow in the footsteps of his father. Vivian then added, "But too much had already transpired. John Jr. had been cursed at too much. He had been left alone too often and worked too hard. He didn't want any part of it."

Miller was the first that I recall to report on kickback schemes involving Price. She provided details about how Price complained that there were no minority contractors being used for the construction of the Frank Crowley building. No one had a clue that there was an ulterior motive behind Price's insistence that Dallas County engage minority contractors. The Crowley Courthouse construction started around 1984. One of the larger contracts went to Dikita Engineering. The contract for civil engineering reached almost three quarters of a million dollars. An African American by the name of Lucious Williams owned the company. The Crowley Courthouse construction was located on the site adjoining the Lew Sterrett Jail.

Price was responsible for increasing minority contracting. And it appears that he hadn't forgotten that fact. Project representative Bill Grimes would frequently tell all contractors that if anything unusual ever happened on the job, he wanted to know about it. Williams approached Grimes one day and told him that Price had asked for a $15,000 campaign contribution. Grimes quickly asked, "Well, did you give him a contribution?" Williams stated that he did not. Grimes replied, "Well, good." The district attorney was informed but told officials that unless Williams would come forward and provide a written statement that nothing would be done. Williams felt that this would only provide fuel to the near riots already taking place across Dallas.

Miller, on more than one occasion, reported about the pickets, threats, and boycotts that Price was involved in. There were several over a period of time. Southwestern Bell Telephone Company managed to experience his "hustle" on more than one occasion. They had published a phone directory with an African-American boy talking over tin cans connected by a string. Price was outraged. Officials with SWB offered to hire a minority contractor in order to make their problems disappear. That company was Spere Cable. When it came time to renew the contract, the owner of Spere complained that Price was charging her an annual fee. She asked Bell officials to not let Price know that her contract was renewed. On another occasion, Price suggested that Bell apply for Exxon credit cards. He then recommended that their employees refuel company vehicles at his Oak Cliff Exxon station.

Another minority-owned firm was Apex Securities, Inc. The owner of that business said she had been "shaken down" by Price. Apex was a Houston investment banking firm that co-managed at least four Dallas County bond issues. Behind the scenes problems surfaced after a shouting match erupted during a commissioners meeting. A company official reported that the real issue was not that Price wanted a slice of the pie from minority contractors. Their concern was that he wanted it for himself. Apex officials finally agreed to hold a political fundraiser for Price. After the event ended, Price received more than $8,000. He wanted more the following year.

Fox and other elected officials began pulling away from Price. He had become too radical. This period of time around the courthouse was known as "The Days of Rage." The charge stemmed from painting over the freeway billboard in south Dallas. It all started when District Attorney John Vance decided to charge JWP with a felony instead of a lesser charge. Price was expecting the misdemeanor charge, but not a felony. He instinctively knew that a felony conviction would require his resignation.

Price was quoted as saying, "Just the mention of John Vance enrages me."

His daily outbursts were frequently referred to as "roid rage." One report mentions that it would be another four years before they subsided.

CHAPTER 10

# The Inner Circle

John Wiley Price has always enjoyed being at the center of attention. He and his radio talk show friend, Willis Johnson, had both been affiliated with KKDA radio station for years. Their years of friendship would eventually weave itself into a web that would take federal agents years to untangle. KKDA was just a tiny little radio station that catered mostly to the African-American community in southern Dallas. It served Johnson well, though. It was his springboard to becoming a sought-after political campaign manager.

Price was also a talk show host on the same AM station. His program, about one hour in length, ran five times weekly. Johnson had developed a devout following with the religious-leaning members of south Dallas. This included most of the powerful ministers of the black churches throughout Dallas County. Johnson had started with the radio station back in 1976. Politicians and ministers of the south Dallas churches were soon regular features on his program. They gloried in the free publicity. Willis certainly enjoyed adding personal contacts to his ever-growing list of politicians.

Kathy Nealy, Price's long-time operative, had always managed the municipal bond election campaign for the City of Dallas. That was until 2006. Lynn Flint Shaw was one of the well-known south Dallas leaders. Officials knew that the bond program would not be successful unless voters from south Dallas were onboard. Shaw asked Johnson if he would like to be the consultant for the bond program. Willis Johnson agreed, and Shaw soon presented the nomination to the full board.

Rufus Shaw, her husband, was greatly pleased that his wife had selected Johnson to work on the campaign. He had been quietly working to push John Wiley Price out of office for years. Her husband felt that this would be the perfect opportunity to move in that direction. Shaw even thought that he could groom Johnson to become the new leader of southern Dallas County. Johnson and Price were good friends, and Johnson didn't seem to be aware of Shaw's ulterior motive.

Price was joined at the hip with Kathy Nealy. He had always made certain that she received the bond-consulting contracts in the past. Nealy was clearly unhappy that this time it would be Lynn Flint Shaw. Shaw had the necessary support from the chair and other members. Willis Johnson would receive the contract. He had already lined up influential minister Frederick Haynes from Friendship Baptist Church. It was now clear that Nealy was out of the loop on this one.

Johnson was paid $30,000 for his work. The program was a success, and program chair Carol Reed could not have been happier. In fact, she was so happy that she thought Johnson should run the south Dallas arm of mayoral candidate Tom Leppert's campaign. It was a hard-fought battle and ended in a runoff between Leppert and Dallas City Councilperson Ed Oakley. The runoff was even more hard-fought. Oakley certainly had ties to south Dallas, but Johnson had deeper ties. He was able to get ministers from the large south Dallas churches to turn out their voters. They showed up at the polls on Super Sunday by the carload. Tom Leppert was now the new mayor, and Willis Johnson's political clout was suddenly off the chart.

Lynn Flint Shaw now placed all of her confidence in Willis Johnson. She had previously acted as the go-to person for minority contracts with the city of Dallas. She now wanted Johnson to fulfill that role. She promptly sent off an email to the new mayor. He was instructed to make certain that Johnson was now the go-to person for all things southern sector and African American. In her email she wrote, "No one, and I mean no one is to go around him. That includes, John Price, Royce West, Don Hill or Ron Kirk. Or anyone else. They all filter through him."

Shaw had been appointed to serve as a board member of Dallas Area Rapid Transit (DART) in 2003. She was later appointed as chair of that board. She introduced an amendment for a security services contract in 2007 that added Willis Johnson and an additional $250,000 to the contract. His name had not been on the original contract. It was later discovered that Johnson had received contracts totaling more than $1.4 million while Shaw served on the board.

Serious concerns over budget shortfalls were beginning to surface in early 2008. Lynn Flint Shaw quietly resigned. But she had more serious problems looming. According to the Dallas County DA's office, Shaw owed Tifany Cheatham $3,500. Instead of paying the debt, she mailed an empty envelop to Cheatham. When contacted, Shaw told her that the check had been stolen. She said that the DA was working on the case. Shaw also told her that she would send her a letter shortly from the DA that confirmed everything. It appears that Shaw then forged a letter from the DA's office and faxed it over to Cheatham. That document was then turned over to the DA and an arrest warrant was soon issued. Shaw was then arrested.

But she had already created a group that would serve as the go-to source between the City of Dallas and minority contractors. This group was secretly known as the Inner Circle. Shaw and Johnson continued working closely together until rumors surfaced that they were receiving kickback money. Those close to Shaw were now concerned that they were leaving an electronic trail that could lead investigators to their scheme.

It was around 6:00 p.m. on March 10, 2008, that Rufus Shaw made two phone calls. One was to his son and the other was to Senator Royce West. Neither answered the phone. The son was out of town playing basketball at the time. It would be several hours before he received the message. He immediately called a family relative, who rushed over to the parents' home. The relative was unable to gain entry to the house. Both cars were parked in the driveway. All the lights were on, and dinner was on the table. A call was made to 911. Paramedics soon arrived and found the couple in the back bedroom. They were both dead.

It appeared that Rufus had shot his wife and then himself. And now Willis Johnson would serve as sole leader of the Inner Circle. We do know that Johnson and Price were working together in 2005. You may mistakenly believe that Ross Jr. only recently entered the picture. It turns out though that Price, Ross Jr., and Johnson were actually working together as far back as 2003.

Willis Johnson had formed a company known as Wai-Wize, LLP, which was listed as a minority-owned telecommunications integrator. Perot Systems, Inc. was about to receive a $140 million contract to take over Parkland Hospital's IT system. There was a serious problem on the horizon. Perot's company was not registered as a minority contractor. Wai-Wize was then brought in as a subcontractor for Perot. As previously mentioned, Price had his hand in as many facets of Dallas County government as possible. That included Parkland Hospital. He controlled that board just as he had controlled the Bail Bond Board. Wade Emmert pointed out that Parkland's board is appointed by county commissioners, and Price had appointed the board's chair. She was completely loyal. A longtime Price associate stated, "John nearly destroyed Dr. McDonald and her practice." Dr. Ron Anderson had been Parkland's chief executive officer for thirty years. He had brought the hospital from a struggling medical facility to become nationally recognized.

But suddenly Dr. Anderson was just like all the others that previously opposed the commissioner's agenda. Price no longer wanted Anderson serving as Parkland's CEO. I was already aware that Dr. Anderson had serious concerns about his future. He had previously confided in me about those fears, specifically over a no-bid contract. The contract that had gone to Willis Johnson. In general, no-bid contracts are acceptable only when the contracts are for professional services, such as legal services.

No-bid contracts were never intended to be used for the installation of a phone system, especially if it would line the pockets of a public official. As soon as the commissioner discovered Dr. Anderson's heartburn over the no-bid contract with Willis Johnson, the war was on. Dr. Anderson's wife later reported that he died from a broken heart.

This was just the tip of the iceberg. I was also having heartburn over one of the Wai-Wize contracts. This one dated back to 2002. The company was paid $100,000 to "evaluate" county communications during a potential terrorist attack. Wai-Wize received an additional $173,000 in 2005 for the development of a satellite communications system, a system that could be used by the county health department in the event of an emergency. Willis Johnson's company was awarded the contract even though its bid was $73,000 higher than that of the competition.

It was a real thorn in my side when I discovered that there was also an annual maintenance fee that ran between $40,000 and $70,000. I began asking questions and was told that part of the fee was for storage. So I asked where the equipment was being stored. It was soon revealed the equipment was being housed at a public storage facility near Mockingbird Lane. There had never a contract for the annual maintenance. It was being renewed under a loophole in state law that permitted professional service contracts to be entered into without a contract.

This sham continued until late 2010, when I called purchasing manager Shannon Brown to my office and asked for an explanation of details. Two days went by without hearing from her. So I called her back to my office. She then began to fill me in on the details. It was now becoming clear that a certain commissioner also had her under his control. The next day, I explained to Brown that this type of communication service could be obtained from any major cell phone provider. Then I mentioned that the going rate would be close to $55 per month. It appeared that she was concerned about going against the commissioner. The item was removed only after I promised to ask questions in open court with the news media present.

The difference in my position and all those that had previously opposed Price was that I had been elected to a four-year term. It wasn't that Price didn't want me gone. He had quickly made that perfectly clear. He and West even asked attorney Greer Raggio, son of legendary prosecutor Louise Raggio, to oppose me in the next election. Greer later declined. Their next pick would be Clay Jenkins. I will never forget the first time that Jenkins spoke at a political event. He started off with "We all know that I have a learning disability." I don't believe that I ever saw his wife angrier.

One of the shams that greatly concerned me was KwanzaaFest. It was always out in the open. There was never any attempt to hide the fact that county employees were working on the event while on the payroll. Price claimed full credit for creating the annual event. It was held in a rented high school hallway the first year. Less than 500 attended at its inception back in 1991. Price then claimed that more than 500,000 have attended every year for the last 15 years. It was advertised as a community health fair.

The event was free. County health officials were providing free screening services for thousands of low-income residents. So, what could possibly be wrong with such an event? Oh, and I would be remiss if I failed to mention that they also contributed around $950 to a scholarship for high school students. The company had been set up under the guise of a nonprofit 501c3 organization. So how did such an event raise money? There was a long list of corporate sponsors. Almost all were well-known corporations. But sadly, the vast majority of the funds were distributed among its board members.

KwanzaaFest lined the pockets of Price and Fain for 24 years. It would be canceled in 2016. Price claimed that the main reason for canceling would be a shortage of volunteers. Actually, it had been discovered that many of those volunteers were on Dallas County's payroll. It was also believed that the weight of a pending federal corruption trial had dried up most of the corporate donations. I do want to mention that nonprofit organizations are required to provide a copy of their financial statement if requested. Price refused to provide that statement. His attorney sent a letter to that effect. A copy was eventually provided by the IRS. Expenses were then made clear.

CHAPTER 11

# Constable Scandal

One of my objectives was to be creative and find common ground that would allow public officials to work together. I was pleased to have made a major breakthrough in that direction. County law enforcement consisted of five constables in addition to the sheriff. Each had separate dispatchers. All six had signed an official memorandum of understanding. A building would be constructed with new state-of-the-art communication equipment. There would be a central dispatch under direction of the sheriff. The court administrator suggested that I, along with the sheriff and constables, pose for a photo with the signed agreement.

It was a short-lived victory. A central dispatch was never built. A short time later, one of the deputy constables was delivering some papers and asked if he could visit with me. I invited him in but instinctively knew where we were headed. He wasted no time in explaining what I thought was a very serious problem. I promised him that someone would soon be in contact. He then left. I phoned the director of human resources. Dr. Taylor assured me that she would contact the deputy.

She explained that other employees also felt threatened. She arranged a group meeting at an undisclosed location, since they all feared retaliation. A total of fourteen deputies attended. She asked each of them to write down their concern. Dr. Taylor came to my office the next day with signed written statements. The complaints were numerous. Some appeared serious. Some even appeared criminal.

One of the complaints that lingered in the back of my mind was from a female deputy with small children. She stated that her constable required employees to make a donation to his campaign fund. She made the donation in order to keep her job. She then wasn't able to buy Christmas presents for her children. I read each and every complaint. Then I called Assistant DA Bob Schell to my office. All the complaints were then turned over to him. I asked that he personally contact the Public Integrity Unit of the DA's office.

Two days later, I called. Schell told me he was still reviewing the complaints. It appears that he had shared those complaints with Price. Both constables were in his district. Price even showed up at a meeting called by one of the constables. He then walked up in front and looked out over the assembled group. "Some of you guys are complaining. You are lucky to have a job. If you don't want to follow orders and pull you weight, then your need to find another job. It's that simple," Price told the deputies.

Another call was made to Bob Schell the following week. He went on to mention that all complaints had been turned over to the DA. He then told me that the matter was now out of his hands. About two weeks later, District Attorney Craig Watkins, Sheriff Valdez, and I met for lunch. I specifically asked Watkins if he was looking into the constable complaints. He replied that he was but refused to provide any details. He added, "I am the district attorney, and this is completely off limits since it could be under investigation."

His response sent a bolt of lightning through my body. Completely shocked, I looked him square in the eye. "Yes, you are the district attorney. I am the county judge, the CEO of Dallas County. You owe me an explanation." Watkins turned his head. He completely ignored me during the remainder of lunch. Two months would pass before I would hear from Watkins again. He called my office wanting to set up a meeting. A meeting was scheduled later that week. He pretended to be interested in discussing the constable investigation.

Once in my office, I explained that the constable investigation remained urgent. I then explained the number of complaints continued to grow. I told him that they had almost doubled. Then I told him that the deputies were losing confidence that I was going to be able to help them. Watkins became angry. He said, "I am not here to discuss the constables. I am here to discuss my budget cuts." I promptly let him know that those concerns needed to be addressed in front of the full court with staff present. Watkins then stood up and quickly headed out the door. It was now apparent that he had no intention of conducting an investigation. Precinct 1 Constable Evans and Precinct 5 Constable Cortes would be free to continue their unethical tactics.

It was now clear that Price, and not Watkins, was driving the bus. I then scheduled a meeting with the Texas Rangers at their district office in Garland, Texas. Commissioner Maurine Dickey and Commissioner Kenneth Mayfield agreed to join me for the meeting. Getting the meeting scheduled was somewhat difficult. Rangers are not eager to become involved in matters involving a district attorney. They are completely dependent on DAs to prosecute their cases.

About two weeks later we met Captain Bryant D. Wells of Company B of the Texas Rangers in Garland. I presented Captain Wells with an outline. The concerns were numerous. Some of the concerns were that the DA had a list of signed, formal complaints. He had refused to investigate those complaints. It also appeared that details of those complaints were leaking out. Employees were being retaliated against. Some were required to work off-duty without compensation. Others were subjected to official oppression.

Captain Wells appeared to be genuinely concerned. He explained that he would evaluate the matter. He even promised to call after his superiors in Austin, Texas had reviewed the details. After all, the Texas Rangers are the highest level of law enforcement in the state. Their slogan is "One riot, one ranger." Two weeks would pass. Then I received the anticipated phone call. Wells explained that all their cases are filed locally. He then told me that they are completely dependent upon local district attorneys. He went on to say that even if they did investigate and charges were brought against the constables, it would be Watkins that made a final decision. State officials felt that their reputation with Watkins would be tarnished if they stepped in. The captain then wished me well.

It appeared as if there was only one possible hope now. That would involve making a trip to Austin. I needed to schedule an appointment with the Texas Attorney General. Getting that appointment was difficult. It would be nearly a month before the meeting would take place. Commissioner Mayfield agreed to join me. We spent close to an hour laying out all of our facts, details, and concerns. We even left a large envelope with all the complaints so that the assistant AG could review the case in full. It would be a month before I heard back.

The Dallas County District Attorney had received an offer from the Texas AG to take over the investigation. After all, it would not be the first time a Dallas County constable had been investigated by the AG. Price urged the previous investigation to move forward, but he was completely opposed to this investigation. I had the item placed on the agenda for the next closed session. Members, under oath, cannot discuss matters considered during closed session. But I can mention details of events that later transpired.

I'm not sure why, but Commissioner Mike Cantrell lined up with Price. They were both adamantly opposed to any investigation involving Evans or Cortes. Constables are required to post a performance bond with Dallas County. An item was placed on the agenda to increase the bond for Evans and Cortes. It passed. Both constables bitterly complained but posted the required bond. Another, but more complicated, item was then placed on the agenda. The item would specifically allow the court to hire an outside investigator to dig into the constable allegation. It passed. Price was livid. Watkins was clearly not happy. He was fuming.

Watkins publicly stated, "Foster has no authority to hire an investigator. It would interfere with a criminal investigation by this office, if there is one." Evans was also unhappy. He was quoted by Kevin Krause of the *Dallas Morning News* as saying, "I have done nothing wrong. Foster should have done his homework before making allegations. So, I think I'll just get me an attorney and deal with Judge Foster on this."

Price vowed to use every source available in order to block an outside investigation. One has to really wonder how deep Price could have been into the operation if he were so adamantly opposed. I felt once the investigation had been completed that everything would come into focus. And it did. I even went so far as to call a former neighbor of Evans. Her name was Dorothy Dean. She had previously mentioned that she was like a mother to Derick Evans when he was growing up. He even played with her children. I explained some of my obvious concerns. She stated that she would talk to him and get back with me. A few days later she called. "Well, Derick stopped by around lunch today. He was driving his police car. I said, 'Derick, you know better. Why are you doing all these things?' He told me, 'Miss Dean, I've got two kids in college. I promise you that I'll turn all this around as soon as they graduate,'" she told me.

Price and Cantrell joined Watkins in their fight against an outside investigator. Price claimed that an assistant DA advised him that the court had no authority to hire an investigator. I felt that we did. We then hired an outside attorney to advise us on the legality of this matter. Well-known attorney Sidney Davis Jr. was hired to deliver an opinion to the full court as to whether an investigator could legally be hired. Once again, Price was adamantly opposed. The plan was to have Davis advise as to how the investigation could proceed as it advanced.

A contract was then entered into that would allow for the hiring of former FBI agent Danny Defenbaugh. He would finally become an investigator that would search for the truth. The next morning my executive assistant delivered the startling details. The 54-year-old attorney Sidney Davis had died earlier that morning as a result of the H1N1 flu. The news was devastating. He left a wife and three children behind.

Evans hired State Senator Royce West to represent him. West is both an attorney and state senator. There was a short period of time that Watkins claimed that he was investigating the constables. So the scenario developed where Watkins was theoretically investigating Evans. Evans hired West to represent him. Campaign records show that West gave Watkins more than $32,000 during his 2006 campaign.

County constables were gradually permitted to operate more and more county vehicles. Those new vehicles were outfitted with full police equipment. More traffic stops were being made. The number of traffic tickets had surged to an all-time high. Those tickets were filed in one of the ten justice of the peace (JP) courts. As the numbers surged, Price began to push for creating a central collections division. He claimed it would accumulate all the tickets in one location. It would free up the JP courts.

He was successful, and the Central Collections Office was set up at the North Dallas County Government Center. Several of the justice court judges complained, especially since some clerk, unknown to them, was using a rubber stamp with the judge's signature and court number. Research revealed that it was the only county-operated central ticket collections operation in the entire state of Texas.

As time went on, I would receive complaints from various citizens about showing up at JP court to pay their fine. After a lengthy wait, they were told that the court had no record of a ticket by that number. The concern was that they would be stopped one day and arrested for failure to pay their ticket. I, along with the JPs, continued receiving those complaints. Central Ticket Collections was in Commissioner Dickey's district. She and I decided to make an unannounced visit to that office in June of 2008.

We were shocked at what we saw. I photographed row after row and box after box of traffic tickets that had never been entered into our database. I then knew the reason behind those complaints.

Commissioner Dickey convened a meeting with the judges of the JP courts. It was agreed that I would lead a transition team that would create a means for moving the tickets back to the various JP courts. Once again Price was livid. I soon realized that we were getting in the way of the money. It was now apparent. Tickets were being left out of the system on purpose.

Row after row of traffic tickets never entered into county database. June 2008, Photo by Jim Foster

Once the tickets reached a certain age they could not be entered into the system and would be turned over to a collection agency. All Dallas County debt collections were turned over to Linebarger Goggan Blair & Sampson. I do know that DeMetris Sampson was a personal friend of Price. She was also named in the June 2011 search warrant executed on the home of Price. Campaign records indicate that her annual contributions to Price totaled at least $10,000.

Former FBI Agent Danny Defenbaugh was now getting deeper into his investigation. He became known to the news media during the bombing of the Murrah Building in Oklahoma City. No question that he was highly qualified. But Price was now angrier than ever. He instructed County Auditor Virginia Porter to hold up any and all payments to Defenbaugh. She complied with his demand.

It was a chilly October evening when someone pressed the button on my door chime. Just as the door opened, I could see a woman wearing a light jacket. Her gun and badge were clearly visible. We barely made eye contact before she said, "Judge Foster, I am with the Dallas County District Attorney's office, and I have a grand jury subpoena. You are to appear at 1:00 p.m. on October 14, 2009." Defenbaugh was also subpoenaed. It was now apparent that Watkins was either trying to indict us or scare us. Neither Defenbaugh nor myself would let up.

Suddenly, Watkins pretended to be conducting an investigation of the constables. But he would never say if he was or was not. Then he threatened Defenbaugh with grand jury scrutiny if he got into the middle of his investigation. He then threatened to charge him with obstruction of justice. That's when an attorney by the name of Lisa Blue Baron entered the picture. Many of you know her as the former psychologist that became an attorney, specializing in jury selection. She had been married to the late Fred Baron, a famous litigator.

I never did understand why Watkins would bring in a private attorney to join him in filing an injunction. But he did. He sued me, Mayfield, Dickey, and Defenbaugh. Was it because her husband had been a symbol of the Dallas County Democratic Party? No one has ever been able to explain that one. In one interview, Blue stated that she and Houston attorney Mark Lanier represented Watkins in his attempt to block the investigation. She then went on to say that she had been sworn in as a special prosecutor. Mark Stanley, prominent Dallas lawyer, stated that he felt that Watkins had let his relationship with Blue affect his judgement. Watkins withdrew his suit a few weeks later.

One deputy's complaint involved his being reprimanded for canceling a call for a tow truck. It appeared that the constable had a verbal policy against canceling a tow truck once the call had been made. The deputy explained that the woman had two small children. It was the middle of July. Outside thermometers were approaching 100 degrees. The woman had no phone and no money and would have had to carry the children to her mother's home about five miles away. His reasoning was completely ignored, and a reprimand was inserted into his file folder.

Of course, my antenna went up. Bells started ringing. Then a constable from another precinct confided in me that he had also been approached by Milad Nasrallah. He told me that Nasrallah, owner of Dowdy Ferry Towing, had offered him $25 under the table for every car towed. He refused the offer. A friend then offered to take some aerial photos of the operation. One quick look at those photos, and the scheme became crystal clear. The photo revealed acres and acres of automobiles.

Constables Evans and Cortes were in the towing business. Both had strict policies on towing. Every driver must show proof of insurance. No insurance and the car will be towed. There was no exception. I contacted Dallas County Auditor Virginia Porter. My concerns were explained. Then I ask when she had last conducted a routine audit of their office. She stated that it had been quite some time. She agreed to select one of the two offices and send staff members out for an audit. I contacted her after the audit, and she stated that she would provide details of the results in open court after the findings were finalized. Those results were never made public. I did learn later that she had sent a detailed report over to District Attorney Watkins's office in February of 2008. Watkins at first denied ever receiving the report. He later admitted that he had received the documents.

The big bucks were adding up. Both Evans and Cortes had numerous traffic deputies, and each made numerous traffic stops daily. The pathetic reality was that almost every automobile that got towed belonged to a poverty-stricken African American or Mexican American. Almost none would be able to pay the towing and storage fee, which was exactly what Nasrallah had hoped for. He was more interested in getting possession of their automobile than he was in the towing fee.

An exact count of towed vehicles was not possible. Some had gone to a salvage yard owned by Nasrallah in Irving. Those vehicles were stripped down and sold for parts. The remaining shell was then sold for scrap. The city of Irving filed an injunction against that operation, and it was shut down. Irving police then filed charges against Milad Nasrallah Jr. for using his tow truck during the night to steal automobiles. That case lingered with DA Watkins for years. Kevin Krause, a *Dallas Morning News* reporter, asked why the case had not been prosecuted. A spokesperson for the DA told him they were no longer able to locate the file.

It appears that at least 13,000 automobiles were towed, all without supervision or oversight by either constable. Once they were towed, neither Evans nor Cortes had a clue as to what happened to that vehicle. Nasrallah was required to report any unclaimed automobile to local police. He had failed to file those reports. He was also required to pay the state a $10 fee for each unclaimed automobile. It appears that he had also neglected to pay that fee. The total would have been around $130,000. I contacted the Texas Department of Licensing and Regulation (TDLR) in an effort to end this scam.

State inspector DeLisa Hamilton was assigned to the case. She called my office one day and asked why I thought there were so many vehicles stored at the Dowdy Ferry location. I explained that I have an aerial photo of the operation. She then told me that those vehicles are no longer there. I asked if she could walk to the main entrance and then turn left and go down until she passed the third gate and walk out into the pasture. She called back and reported nothing was in the pasture. That's when I explained that they were hidden behind a large grove of trees. She called back a few minutes later. Bingo. We had a winner.

Defenbaugh had sent an invoice for a portion of his work. Virginia Porter was holding up the payment. Her original instructions to hold the payment came from Price. She was told in open court that the payment had been approved by the court. She was then asked why the payment was being held. She replied that the DA had instructed her to hold up the payment. This was on Tuesday, December 1, 2009. Price was adamantly protesting payment of the invoice. Mayfield interrupted him. Price went into a rage. It was all captured by a cameraman with KKTV channel 11. It would be referred to as the shot heard around the world. Most of what Price yelled had to be censored. Every other word was bleeped. I loudly banged the gavel and then loudly instructed them to come to order. Price drew back his fist and almost hit the side of my face. He then slammed his fist down on the dais. He leaned over just inches from my ear and shouted, "Make me come to order." Porter continued to hold up the payment until another outside attorney was hired. It would be another 30 days before the invoice was paid.

A deputy contacted me. They needed a meeting place to discuss how to proceed. I offered my office in Oak Cliff. Ten minutes later, Cortes was in the parking lot. I walked over to the door just to make certain that he knew I saw him. He quickly sped away. Time passed slowly. Especially for the complaining deputies. They were losing hope. The entire inquiry took a strange twist on June 3, 2010. An inmate in Collin County jail claimed to know intimate details about the Dallas County constable investigation. Gale Hutchinson, a 44-year-old man with a history of mental illness, told detectives that the constable investigator was plotting to fabricate lies about DA Watkins. Collin County officials, out of an abundance of caution, contacted Watkins's office. They related the sequence of events.

It was as if through the clouds a bright light was suddenly shining. Watkins quickly seized the moment. He realized that he could gain favor by appointing a special prosecutor. He then appointed Ted B. Lyon as special prosecutor. Lyon now had responsibility of reviewing the independent investigator's report. He would also be responsible for uncovering additional information. Lyon was a personal injury attorney in Mesquite. Watkins asked Judge Don Adams to swear Lyon in with full powers of investigation.

Watkins would be harshly criticized after Lyon's appointment. The reality was that Watkins sat on credible information for two years. Cortes would now reveal that he had received a letter from Hutchinson. The letter made claims that Defenbaugh was conspiring in a plot against both Cortes and Watkins. Cortes would now publicly reveal that he had also received a letter from Hutchinson. Cortes claimed that the letter contained details of a conspiracy by Defenbaugh.

That letter was turned over to his attorney. Larry Friedman then sent it over to the DA's office. It would probably be the only time during Watkins' eight-year term that a letter from a mentally ill man prompted him to take action of any kind.

Hutchinson had contacted Defenbaugh right after his constable investigation closed. Defenbaugh could clearly see signs of mental instability. He also determined that Hutchinson was wanted by law enforcement. He was trying to cut a deal. Defenbaugh then sent the man over to talk with FBI agents. His claims were totally unfounded.

Lyon went to work contacting witnesses and scheduling interviews with deputies who were not afraid of retaliation. Some deputies had previously experienced retaliation. One was even called in after he entered the front door of a convenience store. He then left through the back door so that he could meet with Defenbaugh.

Cortes sued me, only to later drop the suit. He then filed a petition to have me removed from office. Neither met with success. It was almost sunset one evening when two technicians from the Dallas County IT Department walked into my office. They had several full-page images from a Dallas County computer located in the office of Jaime Cortes. One image was of his new campaign logo. Another was of his campaign budget. Almost all images were campaign related. Most data had been entered by a campaign worker not employed by Dallas County. We had strict policies that did not permit use of county equipment for political purposes.

I called Court Administrator Darryl Martin over. He was not happy. He asked the tech if that hard drive could be duplicated. One tech assured him that it could. Martin then told the two techs, "Since I am in charge of security, I can arrange for someone to let you in. Would you be able to meet a couple of our security officers at that office tomorrow morning around 5:00 A. M.? They will have keys to every door in the building. You can then replace the hard drive."

The entire operation was arranged by Darryl Martin. I was certainly not opposed to his idea. Nor did I attempt to interfere. Cortes immediately recognized that the computer had been moved. It was not in the exact position he left it. Urgent calls were going out to all departments of Dallas County Government, including Darryl Martin. I do not know what he and Cortes discussed. I seriously doubt he told Cortes that it was he who gave the order for an early-morning visit. I do know that Martin called assistant DA Bob Schell and told him to get over to his office immediately. Schell seemed a little shocked that morning.

Cortes filed suit to get the original hard drive returned. He was not successful. The court ruled that the hard drive be sealed and held in the 101st District Court. The investigation of Evans and Cortes was extensive. Their conduct was unbecoming of public officials. However, the Special Prosecutors needed something that they could sell to a jury, something that the jury could relate to. I was shocked that one of the defense attorneys wanted me as a witness on behalf of one of the constables. Surely, they didn't think that I was going to sing the praises of their client.

A trial was set in district court for the removal of Cortes. That trial would not take place. It was exactly 5:09 p.m. on May 12, 2010, that Cortes sent a fax to my office. The message was brief. It simply stated, "To County Judge Jim Foster, Be advised I am tendering my resignation as Constable of Dallas County Precinct 5 effective July 13, 2010." He also sent a copy to the District Attorney and the removal trial was then canceled.

Then on December 1, 2010, radio and TV stations all across the Dallas Metroplex were breaking the news. Both Evans and Cortes were indicted. Two of Evans's deputy constables, Tracey Gulley and Kelvin Holder, were also indicted. They were each charged with one count of Engaging in Organized Crime. It was almost two years later before Evans would be convicted. He was allowed to remain in office but not permitted to be involved in its operation. He was removed from office a few months later.

Special prosecutor Marquette Wolf opened the trial of former Constable Cortes. Her opening statement was intended to capture the jury's attention. "The evidence will be really beyond any doubt that Jaime Cortes by his own hand, under oath, knowingly and intentionally falsified his campaign finance report," she told the juniors. It wasn't that he may have committed more serious crimes, but this is what would resonate with the jury. This is what would stick. Evans was removed from office. Cortes resigned. Price is still being Price. And no, I wasn't the darling of the Democratic Party, but I stood up for the people. I stood up for what I believed in.

CHAPTER 12

# Unconventional Defense Attorney

Price needed a good lawyer. He had been in trouble before but always managed to exercise a certain amount of political muscle, especially over the district attorneys. But it was different this time. He was now facing federal charges. He needed the best attorney Dallas had to offer. His call went out to William "Billy" M. Ravkind. Ravkind was no stranger to high-profile Dallas officials. He had even represented Price in another case. If you were around Dallas in the late 1980s and early 1990s, then you know what I am speaking of.

This was during the time that Price was breaking windshield wipers. Later, he broke a protestor's leg. That was the first time Ravkind represented Price. They were successful, but Ravkind took the case knowing that Price couldn't pay. That was before Ravkind was charging the big bucks. The truth is that Price could have paid the first time around. After all, he was driving an expensive car, wearing expensive suits, and earning a lot of money.

William Morris Ravkind was born at Dallas on March 7, 1935. He was one of three children born to Abe and Edna Ravkind. His father was a salesperson, and his mother became one of the founders of a maternity apparel company that got it started locally but soon became nationally known as Page Boy.

His brother, Dave "Dudy," was born in New York but attended public school in Dallas. Dudy served his country by joining the U.S. Navy. He was inducted at Dallas on January 15, 1945. He was able to remain in the United States, since the war was coming to a close.

Billy graduated from Highland Park School. His ex-wife Leesie was interviewed by the *Dallas Morning News* in 1992. She told the reporter that Billy was very skinny back in those days. All of his high school friends called him "Weasel," she said. Billy went on to attend the University of Texas at Austin.

He then served as 1st lieutenant in the U.S. Army before being discharged in 1965. He then enrolled at Southern Methodist University's Dedman School of Law, where he graduated first in his class. It was then off to Washington, D.C., where he got his legal career started as an attorney in the tax department of the Department of Justice. Robert Kennedy was the U.S. Attorney General at that time.

Billy felt that he had gained valuable experience as a trial lawyer. He never imagined that he would enjoy his work. But he felt as if he had finally found what he was called to do. And that was serving as a trial lawyer. It seemed as if the underdog was always searching for Ravkind. And he seemed to actually enjoy representing them, especially when they received a successful verdict, which was frequently the case.

Ravkind moved back to Dallas after his time with the DOJ. He was soon representing clients in criminal cases. That was his specialty. He was able to draw in jurors to a degree that few other attorneys possess. He could walk into a courtroom, stumble over an extension cord, and have them in his corner before the trial even started. He came across as one of the last remaining true Southern gentlemen.

Jurors loved his Southern charm. But they also loved the way he could dress down a prosecutor in a New York minute. Judges seemed to let him get away with antics that would bring harsh admonishment for other lawyers. Billy loved the attention. He loved being on stage, and the courtroom was his stage.

Paul Coggins, former U.S. Attorney for the Northern District of Texas knew Billy Ravkind. Coggin said that he was just a rookie federal prosecutor when he tried his first case against Ravkind. "Billy was a showboat. On the first day of trial, he walked into the courtroom with a bag of white powder. He walked over to the judge's secretary and dropped the bag on her desk. Ravkind then told the judge that this was his first exhibit. He looked directly toward the jury. Then with as much Southern charm as he could muster, he told the jurors that his client had to be innocent. He told them that he couldn't afford to buy drugs, so he bought a bag of powdered sugar instead," Coggins reported.

Ravkind rocketed to prominence in 1979 when he gained national attention for a murder-for-hire case. His first big-name client was Jamiel "Jimmy" Chgra. The charge was federal, since Chgra had been indicted for murdering a federal judge in San Antonio. Chgra was acquitted, and Ravkind was an overnight success.

He continued to represent high profile figures. Even in Dallas. Al Lipscomb, the south Dallas African-American City Council member, was one of several on that list. Lipscomb had been charged with taking a bribe from Floyd Richards, owner of the

US Marshal leading Jimmy Chgra into federal court.
He was represented by Billy Ravkind.
Photo by Times Staff, March 3, 1980.

Yellow Cab Company. Lipscomb was convicted. Ravkind was
convinced that his conviction was flawed. One of those problems
he felt was caused by an African-American man being judged by
an all-white jury. Ravkind appealed the case and was successful.

Price was no stranger to the high-profile Highland Park
attorney. For some reason, I was scheduled to appear at one
of Price's pretrial hearings. Ravkind recognized me. He looked
me square in the eye and said, "This whole thing is bull. This
is all bull."

His health began to decline. He looked as if the end was near the next time I saw him. He soon needed a wheelchair. It appears that diabetes was causing the majority of his problems. He would not be able to represent Price throughout the trial. There is an interesting dichotomy between the Lipscomb and the Price cases. Both defendants shared two attorneys.

Lipscomb was first represented by attorney Shirley Baccus-Lobel, and then Ravkind. Price was first represented by Ravkind, and then by Shirley Baccus-Lobel. It was as if history was repeating itself. William M. Ravkind died at his home in the Collin County town of Fairview, Texas, on January 29, 2017.

CHAPTER 13

# Loyal Female Associates

For several years I had been hearing about a female art dealer, one who would open her shop most every Sunday so that J. W. Price could make his selection in private. The subject was occasionally discussed with a mutual friend. The topic always surfaced as to the nature of his scheme. We never did break the code. We never learned the reason behind their frequent meetings. The FBI became interested in all the female associates of Price early in the investigation. They soon uncovered the scheme. It was nothing more than money laundering.

It turns out that dealer's name was Karen Manning. Her shop, Millennium 2000, was located in the old Sears & Roebuck building on South Lamar Street. She actually didn't need to unlock the door. Price had his own key. But she did need to be there when Price wrote checks. Those checks were from his campaign account. Manning cashed the checks. According to court records, she was paid $45 per transaction, and the rest of the money went into Price's pocket.

Manning had already cut a deal with prosecutors in exchange for her testimony. She was facing time in federal prison on tax evasion charges. She became an early witness for the government in the Price corruption trial. Once on the stand, she frequently "didn't remember," or "couldn't recall." So, was she another one of Price's loyal associates? Was she afraid of Price? Or was she just another one of Price's loyal and devoted female associates?

Her name was also listed in the FBI's search warrant for Price's Oak Cliff residence. Other female associates mentioned in the warrant were DeMetris Sampson, Regina Watts, Brenda Jackson and Kathy Nealy. Dapheny Fain was not mentioned. But, agents already had a warrant to search her Desoto home and downtown office in the county administration building. One of Price's most loyal, devoted, and longest tenured female associates would be Dapheny Fain. She initially joined Dallas County's Election Department in 1994. A year later, she was working for Price.

Fain's life seemed to change overnight after she met Price. A former Price ally and county official told me that almost everyone felt that Price and Fain were involved in a relationship at one time. The official went on to say, "Why do you think she has that room in her house set up as a shrine to Price? It went on for a long time." Earlier in life, Fain had worked for Dowell Schlumberger and later for a division of EDS, a Perot company. Dapheny Fain, Kathy Nealy, and Christian Lloyd Campbell were also indicted and would stand trial at the same time as Price. Potential witnesses were indicted separately. Some cooperated and some tried to avoid any appearance of cooperation.

It is interesting to note that Fain previously had worked for Schlumberger, a French oil field services company. She had also previously worked for EDS, a Perot family business. Both companies provided witnesses involving kickbacks during the

Price trial. I have often wondered if it were Fain's connections that brought these two companies into the picture. Court documents indicate that only Nealy was mentioned as the operative in those cases.

Christian Campbell was working for Nealy as a consultant. He was also a consultant for Bearing Point. Testimony revealed that Nealy gave Price a check for $7,500 in return for his support in awarding a 2004 contract to Bearing Point. The contract was for digitizing county records. He testified that he gave Kathy Nealy money so that she could buy influence from Price. Schlumberger had almost no experience with government contracts. Nor was the company a major provider of computer services. That contract with Schlumberger was for $43 million dollars.

Nealy was paying Price for his influence. In return Price made certain that the award went to Schlumberger. Even though Campbell was working for Nealy, he had set up his own company. It was known as Campbell Consulting. Now potential bidders could receive two almost identical information packages when bidding on Dallas County contracts. Campbell previously stated that he passed insider information on to his bosses from Nealy. His boss wanted to know if they were the low or high bid. Nealy sent word that Xerox, Inc., was the low bidder. She then mentioned that Schlumberger was in the middle of the road position. Campbell entered a guilty plea in the Price bribery trial.

Later on, Atos took over the computer servicing contract from Schlumberger. Nealy was bitterly complaining that they were not sending their checks for her consulting services. It was a short-lived problem. Atos made history when major computer problems started cropping up in all branches of Dallas County Government. One of the most serious problems was the jail management system. Inmates were suddenly lost. Sheriff department officials were not able to locate inmates. Many were held weeks beyond their intended release date.

Helena Tantillo was indicted in the Bearing Point scheme. She represented Bearing Point, a digital imaging company. That scheme resulted in a kickback to Price for $7,500. Tantillo was charged for lying to FBI agents. She was convicted in an Austin, Texas, court. She claimed that the payment was actually for a charity event held by Commissioner Mike Cantrell. Cantrell testified in that case. It turned out that her claim was completely false. She would have the distinct honor of being the first person convicted of a crime in the Price bribery trial. It was reported that he was getting a little concerned. There was now an indictment in his investigation. Tantillo was sentenced to six months in federal prison.

Both Nealy and Fain were completely loyal to Price. And he to them. Schlumberger was trying to land a contract in Lee County, Florida. Nealy asked Price to send a letter to county officials there. Schlumberger got the contract. Nealy asked for her $25,000 referral fee. Schlumberger refused the payment. Nealy was furious. Price immediately fired off a letter to Schlumberger's president. He made it clear that he expected Nealy to receive the $25,000 "success" fee. A check was sent out express mail.

Being a nightly feature on the local news was nothing new for Kathy Nealy. She made her media debut during the 2010 federal trial of Dallas City Councilperson Don Hill. He had been indicted in 2007 for receiving kickback money involving affordable housing. It was reported that Nealy was also on the take. Her fee was $175 per hour for her efforts toward convincing council members to lean in her client's favor. She then received an additional $20,000 bonus each time her client's project passed the city plan commission or was approved by city council.

Nealy would have also been charged but agreed to testify in exchange for immunity. Her attorneys claimed that her immunity status was never revoked and therefore she had immunity status in the Price bribery trial. As a result, she was never charged in the Price bribery indictments. It was thought that she would be charged later. But she never was.

Brenda Jackson was also listed in the government's search warrant of Price's private residence. She is currently listed as retired chief of customer delivery at Oncor Electric. She appeared to be hidden in the background. But she knows Price well enough to have lent him $25,000. A longtime acquaintance of Price tells me that they were in a serious relationship at one time and that Jackson believed in Price. She trusted him to the point that she almost lost her job with Dallas Power and Light (DPL) during this time.

Another former female associate was Ora Lee Watson. She appears to have been an administrator at North Lake Community College back in 1987. She was listed in one of the FBI affidavits under "Conspiracy to Commit Bankruptcy Fraud." Mention was made of the purchase of Oak Cliff property, but her involvement dates back to the time that Laura Miller was writing an exposé about Price. The story, published in *D Magazine*, ran in 1991. But it almost didn't run. The magazine at that time was owned by American Express. It was analyzed by attorneys for nearly a year before it finally got the green light.

According to Miller, Price and Watson claimed to have adopted a child. It turns out that Watson and Price were in a serious relationship at one time. Price wouldn't admit to it during Miller's interview, but they had actually adopted two children. Watson operated a day care center and Price was driving the bus for her day care. But as time went on, she began to feel that Price was using her. She filed suit against Price to recover her part of the property investment and another suit for child support.

One female associate had this to say about Price; "I don't know what happened to John Price. He is not the person that I knew. When I first met him, he was really interested in helping people. It's as if something changed. He's a totally different person now."

DeMetris Sampson was also listed in the search warrant affidavit. It appears that she is now retired. She was formerly a principal in the law firm of Linebarger Goggan Blair & Sampson. The firm has had a long-term contract for Dallas County's debt collection. She graduated from SMU's Dedman School of Law. I do recall her stopping by my office after I discovered all the boxes of traffic tickets accumulating in a back room. Price had told her that I wanted those tickets placed back in the JP courts. Sampson was not happy. It was a short visit.

Some research has revealed a little-known fact that concerns me. The law firm that Sampson was a principal in was mentioned in a 2015 news release as having a ranch in Menard, Texas. It is known as the 3348 Ranch. Nothing appears unusual about this other than 33.48 is a section of the Texas Tax Code pertaining to debt collection. Another interesting item has come to light. Linebarger claims that their firm was the driving force behind 2003 Texas legislation that allowed legal firms to tack on a 30 percent collection fee for items such as unpaid traffic tickets.

The witness list was published once the trial got under way. Price had twenty names on that list, and DeMetris Sampson was at the top. Another Price witness was listed as former Chief of Police David Brown. Once contacted by reporters, Brown stated that he had no idea why his name would be on that list.

The combined witnesses list, for the defense and the

government, contained more than 170 names. Many were prominent political figures. Others were well-known business leaders, including Ross Perot, Jr. Just because a name was on that list didn't mean that the witness would be called. But it did mean that you were likely to be called. The government's list contained the vast majority of those names. It listed a total of 150 people. I quickly glanced over the list. And yes, my name had been listed as a potential witness for the government.

Former Councilperson Vonciel Hill was listed as a witness for Price. She was expected to testify about the $305,000 Kathy Nealy was paid for work on the Mike Rawlins campaign. Nealy had been hired to rally voters in south Dallas. Rawlins won his election, and attorneys for Price needed someone to testify that he was not actively involved in the campaign.

Kathy Nealy started out as a struggling young widow. She grew up in Hamilton Park. This development got its start in 1954 as an African-American community. Much of the land later became part of the giant Texas Instruments campus. She and her husband, Charles Nealy had three children when he was murdered. The shooter was a seventeen-year-old boy. Police records indicate that they had argued at the home of the boy's mother. It was reported that the argument was about ownership of the pistol. The boy was not indicted. Others have reported that it was a drug deal.

Nealy was struggling to raise three children and make ends meet when she first met John Price. It has been reported that Price took a special interest in Nealy and that the two were romantically involved. With his help, she soon became a well-known political consultant. She made her mark by working on campaigns such as those of Mike Rawlins and Ron Kirk. The government claims she was funneling kickback payments to Price.

CHAPTER 14

# Not the Person
# I Once Knew

The lengthy search for someone that knew John Price before he became the person that we all know has ended. I thought Betty Culbreath could possibly help. So I gave her a call today. She doubts that there is anyone still around that knew him back then. She told me that they have all crossed the river now. Then she went on to tell me about moving to Nacogdoches, Texas, right after she graduated from college. Betty actually thought she could bring racial equality to that town. I'm not sure why she went there.

She ran for the school board. She then ran for the hospital board. It soon became apparent that Nacogdoches was not ready for change. Betty says that she then moved back to Dallas. She was working for the Community Council of Greater Dallas at the Crossroads Community Center, which is now Martin Luther King Community Center. A lady needed help. She was about to lose her home. She was elderly. The house needed repair, and she couldn't pay her taxes.

Culbreath then recalled, "This poor lady desperately needed help. I called every organization that I could think of. No one, and I mean no one, would offer to help that lady. So I called El Centro College and asked if any of the fraternities could help. They called me back and told me that some of the students had volunteered. A group came over the next day and we went to work repairing that lady's home. One of the students was especially helpful. His name was John Price."

Of course, that prompted me to ask two questions. First, What year was this? Second, so you knew Price before he was elected to office? To which she responded, "Yes, that was back in 1971. He was still a student at El Centro College. He was very nice and very helpful. He was just a college student in those days. I didn't see him again for another seven years. Then one day I stopped by Judge Steele's office, and there he was. I didn't know he was working for Judge Steele. He walked up and asked, "Are you Betty White?" That's my married name prior to moving to Nacogdoches. I said, "Yes, I am." He was beginning to grow up, and I didn't recognize him.

He later told me that he was running for constable. So I offered to help on his campaign. I started working on campaigns while I was in college. All my time was volunteered. He lost that race, but later he decided to run for county commissioner. He won this time, and I helped him set up his office. He would call me over to straighten things out with his staff. He really didn't want that responsibility. Then about six months later he asked if I could come in and take charge of his staff, so I did."

I had recently read an article that mentioned Betty Culbreath had been Price's executive assistant. It was only today that I discovered that she knew him prior to his election. I asked if she was there when Laura Miller interviewed Price. "Oh yes,

I was there. I threatened to throw her out of that office. It was disrespectful. John just leaned back in his chair and let her ask more questions. I guess he thought he could outmaneuver her. But she was smart. I didn't believe any of those things that she was accusing John Price of. "The John Price I knew was a hard worker. The man I knew was for the people. She was talking about a completely different person," Betty responded.

Then I asked if she now believes Laura Miller's theory about Price was correct. She responded in a quiet and disappointed voice, "Yes, it is true. I think it is all true. He had changed and I was not aware of it at that time. I was so disappointed."

My next question was about Price's claim that he never missed a day of work. So I asked about the windshield-wiper incident. "Tell me what happened when Price bent the windshield wiper out in front of the Channel 5 News studio? I thought he got 75 days in jail for that. He claims to have never missed a day since his election. Did he get locked up?"

"Yes, he was found guilty," Culbreath replied. "The news media were all out in front of the courthouse when the verdict came down. He was sentenced to 75 days in jail. I think he served only 30 days or so. He was out all during that time. I know he was in jail, because I went to visit him there. I would take the court agenda and any other documents he needed to the jail. I was working for him back then."

Culbreath continued. She told me that the County Welfare office and the County Health office had previously been two separate departments until County Judge Lee Jackson asked that they be combined. Culbreath was then asked if the job were offered as Director of Health and Human Services, would she take it?

She responded that she would. Each of the four commissioners would then meet with her. Each had their own list of different concerns and questions. The first question from Commissioner Nancy Judy was "Will you stand up to John Wiley Price?" To which Culbreath responded, "Yes, I sure will." That was what Nancy Judy wanted to hear.

Culbreath didn't experience any problems from Price for the first couple of years. She said as time went on, he wanted to manage her department, telling her whom to hire and whom to fire. He gradually wanted complete control. She resisted. All department administrators were required to be present every Tuesday for commissioners' court. Price would turn all items pertaining to her department into major issues—anything on the agenda pertaining to Health and Human Services. It didn't matter how minor it was. He acted then just as he acts now. He wanted to be in complete control.

Eventually Culbreath needed a kidney transplant. She was under a lot of stress, and Price seemed to hone in on that. She spent about three months recovering. The first day of her return, she happened to look at the court agenda. There it was. The first item on the agenda mentioned her replacement. She called Court Administrator Allen Clemson and asked why her replacement was on the court agenda. Allen replied, "Well, they want you to resign. You need to turn in your resignation."

Culbreath was shocked. She sent off a fax to the news media. One of the reporters picked up on the story. The next day there it was in bold print. "Dallas County Commissioners want Director of Health and Human Services resignation." The article went on to mention that she received word on her first day back to work. She had been out for three months recovering from a kidney transplant. The article went on to mention that "Ms.

Culbreath, under pressure from commissioners, has tendered her resignation, which will take effect in six months."

Price was furious. He instructed Clemson to find a way to get her out of the picture. Culbreath refused to bow down. Her office was located over on Stemmons Freeway. Price wanted the new director, Zachery Thompson, in that office. Price instructed Clemson to move Culbreath out of her office. She was then relocated to a small cubicle on the third floor of the county administration building on Elm Street. She didn't even have an office phone, only an old metal desk and a worn-out chair.

Price continued to pressure Clemson. He finally instructed Clemson to get her out immediately. Clemson showed up at her metal desk and explained that she needed to go and that she would be paid until the end of the month. He took her county-issued cell phone. Her replacement, and Price appointee, Zach Thompson remained in that position for twenty years. He was removed from office after a serious employee complaint in January of 2018. Dallas County Commissioners later awarded that employee a $120,000 settlement.

Laura Miller had referred to Price as "The Hustler." It was only after reviewing that lengthy 1991 article that I discovered why. It appears that Price actually gave himself that title.

He was born April 24, 1950, in the small east Texas county of San Augustine. He, along with his parents, Holman Colman and Willie Faye McCoy Price, soon relocated to Forney, a small Kaufman County town. His father was a truck driver and a part-time preacher. His mother stayed home and took care of the children. Price had bitter feelings about attending segregated schools in Forney.

It was 1968 when he moved into a mostly white neighborhood in Dallas off Dolphin Road near Interstate 30 in 1968. Miller reported that his dream was to land a janitorial job with the Sanger-Harris Department Store at Big Town Shopping Center in Mesquite. His interview was conducted by the store manager. Price would be selling menswear instead of doing custodial work.

A few months later he was transferred to the appliance department, where he was selling high dollar items. He was getting 5 percent commission on every sale. Price said, "The little guys had been there forever. Hell, I was starting to hustle. I was taking their money. I was raking it in. People would come in to look at the stereos, so I would help them. I was aggressive."

It is somewhat ironic that Price is considered to be the leader of south Dallas, a mostly African-American area. One of his associates tells me that he had never been to south Dallas until after being elected county commissioner.

By 1970 Price had enrolled at El Centro College and was married. By 1972 he had been elected a Democratic precinct chair. He supported Senator George McGovern for president. Most of the other delegates in his precinct were white and supported Governor George Wallace. Party rules required Price to cast the majority of his votes for Wallace.

It was at that precinct convention that he first met Al Lipscomb. "Al walked up to me and said, 'Why are you casting your votes for George Wallace?'" Price told a reporter. Then he added that he was just a green kid and didn't know any better.

CHAPTER 15

# The Investigation Concludes

Almost eleven years would pass from the onset of an initial investigation in early 2006 until the first day of trial. Critics of Price complained bitterly. They even expressed doubt that he would ever stand trial. This case was unlike any other ever investigated in Dallas County. It was extremely complex. It was considered to be one of the largest white-collar cases in the history of the FBI. It was certainly the largest case ever tackled in their Dallas office.

Veteran FBI Special Agent Don Sherman was no stranger to white-collar corruption. During his 20 plus years with the bureau, he had been involved in every major corruption investigation targeting public officials in Dallas County. One of his first investigations involved Dallas City Councilpersons Paul Fielding and Al Lipscomb. City councilman Don Hill was next, followed by Texas State Representative Terri Hodge. All were indicted with Sherman's assistance.

But the John Wiley Price investigation was different. The Price case had roots, roots that were embedded deep beneath the surface. The roots that were so widespread they reached into almost every section and cross-section of local government. It would be an investigation so deep that it would shake the bedrock of Dallas County government. Sherman was not assisting in this case. He was now leading one of the FBI's largest squads to ever conduct an investigation in the state of Texas.

Sherman even suggested that a pole camera (a camera placed on a utility pole) be set up to monitor traffic into and out of Price's residence. But Price was a shrewd man and had long been aware that his home was subject to observation. However, even the cleverest people make mistakes, and Price's vulnerability stems from an insatiable desire to brag. He seemed to especially enjoy bragging about how he could beat the system.

He often boasted about breaking a TV camera operator's leg and how he was never convicted. There was, in fact, a long list of various scenarios that he bragged about. One even included a little hometown bank for his "rainy day" fund. In reality, Price would often closely resemble the familiar storybook characters known as Hansel and Gretel. Hansel and Gretel intentionally left a trail of breadcrumbs. Price never intended to leave one shred of evidence—not one hint of a trail. He had no clue that his breadcrumbs would one day attract two monsters, living, breathing monsters with three-letter names. Those monsters that would forever change his life.

Sherman and his highly trained crews were quietly digging deeper and deeper into phone records, bank records, and tax returns. They were following the money trail, and the breadcrumbs would soon lead to three women, women that were devoted enough to willingly launder Price's money. Surely they had to realize the serious repercussions of their actions should they ever be exposed.

Those fears would soon be realized. The IRS and FBI conducted simultaneous raids on their homes and offices in addition to the home and office of Price. Agents were not completely surprised to find a large safe hidden in Price's home. A special crew was called to assist in getting the heavy old-fashioned safe open. An extensive inventory of its contents would soon reveal expensive Rolex watches and other jewelry in addition to more than $220,000 in cash.

Agents searching Fain's home soon found Price's Bentley stashed in her garage. They were not expecting to find a small room in her home that had been arranged as a shrine. Her complete devotion to Price was now evident. It was now clear why she had lied to FBI agents during her questioning about Price earlier that day. Numerous life-size photos, tokens, and other memorabilia clearly demonstrated her faithful devotion. She even displayed a poster-size photo of Price clad in a skimpy swimsuit with his oversized rear end serving as the center of attention.

Dozens of agents had fanned out across town and were busy loading file boxes, computers, and other items into their government-issued SUVs. There was no question that Sherman was in charge. He was downtown, closely monitoring agents as they loaded files from Price's county office into their vehicles. They finally finished their detailed task. Just as they were preparing to leave, Price looked up. He rumbled, "If you guys are finished, maybe I can get back to work now." Sherman was not amused. He responded with "Mr. Price, you don't appear to be taking this very seriously. Perhaps you should realize that today is the first day of the rest of your life."

No one can deny that the FBI, IRS, and Department of Justice conducted a thorough and extensive investigation into the background of the most powerful politician in the history of Dallas County. Many also believe that he is the most vindictive and overtly corrupt politician in the northern district of Texas. It would be almost exactly ten years from commencement of the original investigation before a trial would take place.

A panel of 70 potential jurors was called on the first day of trial. Judge Barbara Lynn was no stranger to cases involving elected officials. She had presided over many. But this one was different. Price and his loyal assistant Dapheny Fain would spend the day watching the jury pool be whittled down. Kathy Nealy had been removed from the case. The courtroom was crowded. News reporters and sketch artists were relegated to the jury box.

Judge Lynn announced that a catering company be called in to provide lunch. She then instructed the defense and prosecution to knock 40 minutes off their allotted time for questioning potential jurors. The judge instructed jurors to pay attention. She told them that they would not know if they were a juror or an alternate juror until the trial ended.

Attorneys for Price had brought in Dr. Jaine Fraser, an expert in jury psychology. Dr. Fraser helped defense attorneys prepare a pretrial questionnaire for potential jurors. She also guided them during the voir dire process and during the trial.

By 9:00 p.m. a jury of twelve, along with four alternates, had been selected. It had been predicted that jury selection would take a full week. Instead, it was accomplished in one very long day. The judge's firm oversight of jury selection had set the stage. It was clear that she would exercise strict control of the trial. Fain could have received leniency in exchange for her cooperation. She refused at least three offers from prosecutors.

Price had bragged about never missing a commissioners meeting since taking office more than 30 years earlier. On the second day of court, his high-back leather chair was noticeably vacant. Most of the local TV news reporters were down at the federal building. The scant few that did show up for the commissioners meeting promptly zoomed in on his vacant chair. It would be the first time his chair remained empty for an extended period of time since his arrest around 1980.

Court convened right on schedule the next morning. Price walked in surrounded by his attorneys. It was the first time in decades that he had walked into a courtroom without a brightly colored bow tie or flashy suit and expensive shoes. His dress more closely resembled attire suitable for a funeral. The jury was barely seated before Judge Lynn sharply snapped her gavel and called court to order. Her usual statements followed, "The United States District Court will come to order. Defendants will rise. Defendant Price, how do you plead? Defendant Fain, how do you plead?" Both responded with "Not guilty."

Prosecutor Katherine Miller began reading the government's 107-page indictment, an indictment so lengthy that it took Miller four hours to read. She quickly pointed out that Price received a check for $1,000 one day, he purchased a BMW the next day, and then purchased land on South Lancaster Road the next day, all with funds from political consultant Kathy Nealy and all in exchange for his favorable vote on a lucrative contract.

Defense attorneys objected. They claimed there was no time left for their presentation about how unfairly government officials had singled out John Wiley Price. Judge Lynn was clearly unhappy. She reluctantly adjourned court early so that opening arguments by both the defense and prosecution could be presented the following morning. One of the jurors also needed to leave to care for an ill parent.

Court convened promptly the following morning with the

prosecution spending the majority of its time focusing on the money trail. It then moved on to the various checking accounts. It pointed out that Price had signature authority on at least four bank accounts. There was his primary account in addition to his Telco Credit Union Checking account. He was also able to sign on Fain's personal account in addition to his mother's account at the bank in Forney. The prosecution made clear that Price's mother didn't even know about the account. She was never listed on the signature card.

County administrator Darryl Martin was called as the prosecution's first witness. He explained that commissioners were prohibited from viewing, sharing, or discussing pending contract information. FBI financial forensic expert David Garcia was called the following day. He spent two days demonstrating how Price, Nealy, and Fain received financial gain from Dallas County contracts. He zeroed in on how lobbyist and political consultant Kathy Nealy received more than $1 million from seven companies seeking Dallas County contracts. He walked over to a large chart that illustrated that most of the money had been funneled to Price. Nealy was even making deposits into his account at the Forney bank.

Garcia then told jurors that Price received more than $550,000 from a company known as Mail Man Sales (MMS), which was operated by Dapheny Fain. Garcia made it clear that Price had close to $230,000 in his safe. His total money was well in excess of $1 million. Defense lawyers claimed early on that the government exceeded the statute of limitations by waiting so long to indict Price. However, the exception was anything in excess of $1 million and it was now clear that Price had exceeded that limit.

Defense attorneys attempted to convince jurors that the money Fain paid to Price was in repayment of loans dating back to

2005. This brought a prompt response from prosecutors. They pointed out the MMS was not even in existence in 2005. They also pointed out that the total paid Price would have been $127,000 in excess of the loan.

Prosecutors then explained to jurors about the financial benefit Price received from art gallery owner Karen Manning. They detailed how Manning paid Price more than $200,000 in an attempt to launder money from his political campaign account. She had already entered a guilty plea and at some point would be called to testify for the prosecution.

On Friday, another alternate juror was dismissed. This left only three alternates. This caused considerable concern from Judge Lynn. The prosecution ended its week with a hard-hitting presentation of confidential emails. All were from county purchasing director Shannon Brown. All were addressed to Price. Brown had suddenly resigned after an FBI interview. She would later appear as a witness for the DOJ.

Brown's email pertained to an open bid for an upcoming high dollar contract with an information technology (IT) company. It is a violation of county policy to share information pertaining to an open bid with employees. That includes commissioners. That email, from Unisys Corporation, should have never been forwarded to Price. But it was. Four days later, Price forwarded the email to Nealy. She then arranged a breakfast meeting with Unisys officials and Price.

Was Shannon Brown part of the hustle, or was she simply afraid of losing her job? It is my humble opinion that it was the latter. If she would have remained in that position for another two or three years, it could have been entirely different story.

CHAPTER 16

# Overheard at the Courthouse

It was not uncommon for me to overhear John Price discussing items that I thought he would have wanted kept confidential. Sometimes I would think he was just tuned out as to my presence. Maybe he didn't realize I was even there. Other times I felt as though he thought I was tuned out. Regardless, I would occasionally overhear him talking about various items that would be forever imprinted deep into my mind.

Some of those items, and not in a specific timeline, will perhaps give you some insight as to his way of thinking. Two of those incidents occurred while on a trip to meet with State Jail Commission officials in Austin, Texas. Court Administrator Darryl Martin had accompanied us. We were standing out in front of the entrance to the commission's office building when a Tarrant County commissioner approached. He explained that Alliance Airport was in his district and that he really needed to speak with Ross Perot, Jr. He then asked if Price could help him get in contact with Ross Jr.

Without giving it one second of thought, Price reached into his pocket and pulled out his phone. He then glanced down at his phone and instantly replied, "Oh here it is. I've got him on speed dial." None of this would be important except it appeared that Price was attempting to kill the 6,000-acre Dallas Logistics Hub. It was widely believed Price was receiving kickback money from Perot. A Dallas area reporter had previously asked Price if he knew Ross Jr. Price responded with, "I have only met him at a few social events. I don't actually know him."

Later in the day, Price, Martin, and I were walking across the parking lot, and for some reason, Price began his proud boast to Martin. The subject centered on a construction worker who had been injured by Price sometime around 1991. In his loud and boisterous voice, laughter rang out as he began to brag to Martin about the event. Price exclaimed, "I broke that joker's leg. You know what they did to me. Nothing. I mean nothing at all." The truth is, the assistant DA in charge of the case told me in later years that she has always regretted not prosecuting Price for his role in that confrontation.

If I needed to visit with Allen Clemson, it was not at all uncommon to discover Price already in his office. There was absolutely no need to walk in if I could hear the two of them in a heated discussion. Such was the case concerning a longtime employee, Nancy Woertendyke

The two items that seem to haunt me most pertain to Nancy Woertendyke and Commissioner Maurine Dickey. Neither subject was intended for my edification. Nor did they initially realize that I was present. But as they used to say, it's too late to close the barn door after the horse is out.

I never did know exactly why Price was unhappy with Nancy Woertendyke. She had worked in several positions and was in charge of the Dallas County Security Department when Price went after her. She was very close to retirement at that time. I had headed over to Clemson's office. Just as I approached the door, Price was raging. "I don't care if that bitch is about to retire. You need to get her out of here. She needs to go," he yelled.

I returned to my office. A few days later it was official. She had been terminated. Sometime later, I was notified that she had sued Dallas County. I was asked to meet with her attorney and an assistant from the DA's office. I spoke the truth, and she was awarded a settlement. None of the money came from JWP's pocket. It was all at the expense of the taxpayers.

After being away from county government for more than ten years, you would think that I would forget about this injustice. But that termination, along with a maintenance worker fired at Price's insistence, continue to linger in my mind. His great sin? He had told his supervisor that someone in an official county vehicle was carrying tools out of Price's Oak Cliff home. The supervisor then called Clemson. And you guessed it, Clemson then called Price. It soon all went downhill.

I was also unhappy about hearing a conversation between Assistant DA Bob Schell and Clemson. It was over an item that pertained to a constable under investigation for employee harassment. Schell wanted the item on the agenda. Clemson loudly protested. "Court starts in thirty minutes. Why are we just now getting this report? We should have had this a week ago," he loudly replied.

At the suggestion of Price, former Judge Mary Ellen Hicks had been hired to investigate Constable Dupree. Her report did not please Schell or Price. Schell then wrote the report himself. He faxed it over to Hicks with instructions that she sign it and return it via fax. Schell, responded, "We just got the fax a few minutes ago." I turned and walked back to my office. It was a hot topic. Every news source wanted to know about the constable's forced resignation.

I refused to comment. To me the bigger story would have been about that document, a document written by one person and signed by another. A document that resulted in official action by the court. Price was in the loop. I accidently discovered the ploy, but the other three members were totally unaware. You may wonder why I didn't just call them to my office for an update. Court members are not permitted to meet with each other unless advanced notice of the meeting has been publicly posted.

Another boast that continues to linger in my mind also was never intended for my ears. I always felt that it was such an injustice, though. I believed that it concerned a vindictive, nefarious act. That boast was addressed to Cantrell. Both Price and Cantrell were unhappy with Commissioner Dickey. Each county in Texas has four commissioners and one judge. The judge presides over the commissioners court. The judge also presides over civil and criminal cases in the smaller counties. That position is countywide. Each commissioner represents a district, and the court is permitted to redraw those districts every ten years if the census indicates a significant shift in population.

It was around 2010 when I overheard Price laughing as he called out to Cantrell. "Hell, she (Dickey) won't even live in her district when we are finished with her. She'll have to walk across the street just to find to her district," Price boasted. It turns out they were right. Price and other court members agreed on new district lines. Those lines changed enough that she could no longer win an election. She had been intentionally gerrymandered out of her district.

Those lines were changed again in 2021. Price is the

commissioner for District 3. I drew a diagonal across a map showing the latest Dallas County districts. I noticed that District 3 covers almost all of the southern sector of Dallas County. It then shoots around through Rowlett and up to the Collin and Rockwall county line. His new district covers almost half of Dallas County. I realize that total population of each district needs to be essentially the same. But at the same time it appears that the original intention is to cancel out the right-leaning voters in the Rowlett area. If my prediction is correct, it will be an exclusively Democratic court within the next four years.

The latest census did indicate that the total number of Dallas County residents has increased over the last ten years. But it has not increased enough to mandate that district lines be redrawn. However, the majority of court members wanted new district lines.

To be honest with you, I know the right-leaning guys do it themselves all the time. But this one doesn't pass the smell test. Price can be charming when he wants to. He can charm the pants off an alligator if it is to his benefit. I watched him as he went out of his way to charm Dickey. But when it came time to vote, she would vote for what she felt was right. And, in my opinion, you shouldn't draw someone out of their district just because they voted against one of your pet projects.

Talking to reporters was an entirely different matter. Price loved to be in front of the cameras. He loved being in the spotlight, especially if he had the opportunity to bash me. October 16, 2009, provided him with just such an opportunity. He had been stewing over a comment that I had made to Jim Schutze with the *Dallas Observer*. It had been almost a year since the story was first printed. And it had stuck in Price's craw ever since.

He went after Congresswoman Johnson and then he went after me. She moved the law suit to federal court and Price was not able to pursue it. He then turned all his ire against me. It actually wasn't a lawsuit. He filed a petition for discovery in Judge Ken Tapscott's County Court at Law. He felt that this would give his attorney ample opportunity to dig into the matter and see if there was a basis for a lawsuit. This was a little-known and rarely used legal maneuver. Tapscott ruled that the deposition could proceed. One of the reporters for WFAA TV picked up on the headline story and the battle was on. Price had the first volley. "I'm looking forward to vetting and grilling. Let's see your evidence. That's what this is about," he told the reporter.

My response was fairly short and to the point. "With the commissioner trying to proceed with this, he's getting ready to open up Pandora's Box," I said. It was a short statement, one that I believed should have sent a fair warning. It was a shot over the bow. Federal agents almost certainly saw the news release. A few days later, one of the agents made it clear that I needed to answer truthfully while under oath, even if the question arises about the investigation.

The question did arise, and I answered truthfully. That's when Pandora's Box swung open wide. Both Price and his attorney seemed shocked. They now realized he was under federal investigation. His obsession about my comment to the *Observer* suddenly paled in comparison. He was no longer obsessed with a comment about shaking down the developer of in inland port. He would now need a different attorney. One that specialized in criminal law.

CHAPTER 17

# Agent Behind the Scenes

It was while on a trip to Austin that I overheard Price bragging about how to avoid being charged with a crime. He stated that as long as someone else was doing your dirty work, you'll never have to worry about it. You'll never be charged with anything. At the time, I didn't believe that to be a true statement. Even believed that I could see through his thinly disguised veil. Looking back, it appears that some of those that did his dirty work have paid. They will suffer endless ridicule, all because they were caught up in the whirlwind of his activities.

One of the first to be charged as a result of the Price corruption investigation was 59-year-old Helena Tantillo. Her ex-lover, Christian Campbell, would later be indicted. Tantillo had made two false statements to FBI agents. The FBI originally investigated her pertaining to a kickback to Price in the amount of $7,500. She falsely claimed the check was for charity.

The jury deliberated for four hours before returning a guilty verdict. Tantillo just sat there, completely motionless, after the judge read her guilty verdict. We do not know if she had been offered immunity in exchange for her cooperation.

Karen Manning was also indicted. She was originally an interior decorator. She had moved into the old Sears and Roebuck building on South Lamar after it was converted into condos. Her original business was in furniture sales, but she began selling art after the move. Once agents presented her with all the facts, she agreed to cooperate. In exchange for a lighter sentence, she offered testimony on behalf of prosecutors in the Price bribery trial. It was thought afterwards that she was not a great witness. She couldn't remember details that she clearly knew firsthand. She had pleaded guilty in 2015. Judge Barbara Lynn ordered Manning to pay $97,309 in back taxes. I'm not sure that she impressed the jury, but she was facing three years in a federal penitentiary.

Christian Campbell had already entered a guilty plea on a federal charge of bribery. He would not be sentenced until after the Price trial. He admitted that he funneled money to Kathy Nealy. That money then ended up in the bank account of John Wiley Price. Campbell had testified on behalf of the prosecution during the Price bribery trial. He received six months probation.

Court documents indicate that Price also held art exhibits in Manning's gallery. A postcard was entered into evidence. The card advertised an "Out of Africa" art exhibit presented by Price. She testified that she marked his art with special tags that read John Wiley Priceless Collection. She wanted everyone to know that the art was from Price. Officials believed that she also cashed checks from his campaign account. Those checks were exchanged for cash. She kept $45 for each transaction.

It would be late 2009 before Price knew he was under FBI investigation. It would have probably taken another year or two had he not sued me. Once the *Dallas Morning News* broke the story, it was all over radio, TV, newspapers, the internet, and every other media outlet. Price attempted to deflect public attention. As cameras began to roll, he stated, "It's just an investigation. No one has been arrested." I interrupted at that point, and clearly stated, "And that's a shame. You should have been." Of course Price instantly became angry. His true self was showing to those watching the nightly news.

The agent behind the scenes was no stranger to official corruption investigations. He had been involved in the majority of Dallas corruption cases for more than twenty years. The list is lengthy. He was right in the middle of the case involving Dallas City Council members Al Lipscomb and Paul Fielding. Later there was the case of Councilman Don Hill and Dallas Planning Commissioner D'Angelo Lee. Next came State Representative Teri Hodge's case. He was a veteran federal investigator. He was known to take his role very seriously and to be a man of few words.

Don Sherman explained how he became an FBI agent during an October 14, 2019, interview with Leah Wietholter. He said that he was in college working on a degree in an accounting when a recruiter first contacted him. "I turned their offer down. I finished college and went on to start my own business. It was a franchise. It became very successful, and I was offered way more than it was actually worth, so I sold it. That's when I applied to the FBI Academy. They actually accepted my application," Sherman explained.

After graduating from the FBI Academy, he was offered his choice of nine different cities he could call home. Sherman explained, "I narrowed that list down to Dallas or Denver. Then I chose Dallas. This was about the time the housing market crashed in 1987 and I couldn't sell my house. So, the move was postponed about six months. I was assigned to a field training officer once I arrived in Dallas. My first case was being tried in San Antonio. I was mostly observing. The training officer was presenting the case. My first case to investigate was actually a spinoff from that one. It was for fraud. That's when I learned how to trace money—how to follow the money. I actually lost that case, but it taught me how to prepare for future trials. I never lost another one after that."

The veteran agent then explained about his Evidence Flow Chart. He went into great detail about how it would be explained at trial. He would then make sure that the jury could take his chart into the jury room. It was becoming crystal clear that this type of oversight was missing from the Price trial.

The host then wanted to know if he would tell about his first high-profile case. Sherman recalled, "I was over in Highland Park when I noticed an expensive BMW parked in an unusual place. I did a double take and wondered why is that expensive car parked there. Then a few days later I received a call about Dallas Mayor Pro-Tem [Don] Hill and that very same BMW. It would lead to a major public corruption investigation at Dallas City Hall. This was in 2004 and I was getting married."

The interviewer then requested details of the initial investigation. Sherman responded, "I needed to get a wiretap set up. There is a lot of paperwork involved just to get a wiretap authorized. I was so busy with that case we couldn't take our honeymoon. There were more than 33,000 phone calls, and every single one had to be transcribed. We traced more than 100,000 bank transactions. When it was over, seven subjects were indicted and all were convicted."

His convictions seemed to be almost always certain. Without

exception, all were convicted. The Lipscomb case was later overturned on appeal, but only after Lipscomb had spent time in federal prison. D'Angelo, Don Hill, and Hill's wife were all convicted in that trial. Sherman was known as the "bulldog." He always got his man. Or woman.

But his world was about to change. Sherman had led the June 27, 2011, downtown raid. He personally supervised every aspect of the FBI and IRS search warrant on Price's office. Sherman was in the hospital about a year later for routine surgery when he suffered a massive stroke. Doctors called in his family. They even told his wife that death was 98 percent likely. Against all odds, he survived. But his world would be forever changed.

The government's role in prosecuting the Price case was also suddenly changed. Normally, the lead agent advises prosecutors on how to proceed. Suddenly, their lead agent was incapacitated. Another agent could be placed in charge, but that agent could not possibly know all the facts and details. All FBI facts in every case are well documented. But it would take a new special agent in charge (SAIC) months to become familiar with every detail, especially in this case since there were more than one million files involved. There is no question that the absence of an SAIC in the Price investigation would significantly impact its progress.

Don Sherman was now dependent upon others. He couldn't drive a car. His entire left side was paralyzed. He couldn't even sit up in bed. It was during the Paul Fielding and Al Lipscomb investigation that he had made an unusual friend. Sherman later stated, "During my 22 years as an agent, it's the only time that I allowed someone under investigation to enter my life. It was while working on that case that I met Roger Hoffman. It was not a pleasant introduction."

Sherman was a young agent working undercover as Don

Shuman. He had previously met Hoffman in the capacity of his undercover role. He showed up at Hoffman's Plano home late one day. He knocked on the door. Hoffman opened the door. He seemed a little surprised. Then Sherman showed him a badge. He went on to ask if he could come in. "It looks like you're in real trouble. I believe that I can help you if you agree to cooperate with this investigation," Sherman told him.

Hoffman was very concerned. He feared for the safety of his family. Sherman assured him that he would help in exchange for his cooperation. "If you help me, I will do everything that I can to protect you," Sherman assured him. Hoffman pled guilty to failure to report a crime. He was sentenced to three years probation in exchange for his role as a witness.

Hoffman's life went into a downward spiral after his conviction. His finances, his marriage, everything seemed to fall apart. He contacted the one person that he believed could help. That person was none other than the one who had arrested him. He made a call to Don Sherman. Hoffman explained his problem in detail and then ask if Sherman could help. Hoffman was totally surprised. It was not the answer he had expected. "Roger, I don't have the answer for you. But I know someone that does. I'll pick you up next Sunday and take you to church with me," Sherman said.

Hoffman had grown up on Long Island, New York. He had been raised in the Jewish faith. Sherman, for some reason, felt that Hoffman would be comfortable attending service at one of the larger Baptist churches in Dallas. It appears that he was correct. Hoffman eventually became a member and was converted to the Baptist faith. Sherman now considers Hoffman his brother. He says that Hoffman was one of the few whom he could depend on when he desperately needed help. He would pick up Sherman, take him to the gym, physical therapy, or any other place he needed to go. They became close friends.

Sherman retired from the FBI in 2013 after the near-fatal stroke. His role as an investigator in the Price case was over. He would be called as a witness once the trial started. It was a cold Tuesday morning in February 2017 when he walked into the Earl Cabell Federal Building in Dallas. He was no stranger to that courtroom. He had been there many times before. But this time he needed a cane to help steady him as he walked over to the witness stand. The oath was administered, and he would soon take his position.

Sherman started out telling about how the investigation had begun. It involved banking transactions that tied political consultant Kathy Nealy to Price and how transactions tied assistant Dapheny Fain to Price. He went on to explain that the purpose of those transactions was to influence Price's favorable vote on county contracts. Those banking transactions totaled in the tens of thousands of dollars, if not in the hundreds of thousands of dollars.

The former special agent in charge then outlined activities during early stages of the investigation. Once the Dallas office received approval from the FBI's Public Corruption Office in Washington, D.C., the FBI began its investigation. "Once we had approval, we poured a tremendous amount of time into watching his home and his cars and looking into his bank accounts," Sherman testified.

Sherman went on to describe his encounter with Fain. "At first she was calm and collected. We needed a private place to talk due to all the activity taking place that day. She even suggested that we go to the commissioners private meeting room. But then she denied any connection between her private business and Price. When it was explained that we have bank records, she became agitated. She then resisted in answering our questions. She then stated that we were just trying to trick her and suddenly ended the meeting. She got up and walked out. All of this was in the County Administration Building," he stated.

Thomas Mills, defense attorney for Fain, would then question Sherman. He seemed to zero in on Sherman's ability to clearly recall details of the investigation. He even asked Sherman if the stroke had affected his memory. Sherman responded, "Any lapse of some minute detail is not a result of the stroke. My memory is good. It would be due to the enormous volume of evidence and the time elapsed since our investigation began."

Sherman had met Tom Mills outside of the courtroom earlier that day. He mistakenly called him Bill instead of Tom. He instantly knew that Mills would likely bring up their casual meeting once on the stand. Mills wasted no time in asking Sherman if he recalled their meeting earlier that day. Sherman assured him that he did. Mills then went on to paint a picture of how the lead FBI agent's memory was fading, how he didn't even know the name of one of the lead defense attorneys.

Price had remained free all during the investigation until Friday, July 25, 2014. He, along with Kathy Nealy, was then arrested by FBI agents. Fain and Campbell turned themselves in. All four were released later that day on personal recognizance bonds.

The trial date had been originally scheduled to begin on January 19, 2016. This was more than a year since Price had first appeared in court. Defense attorneys then petitioned the court to again move the date based on the tremendous amount of evidence collected during the investigation. More than 9 terabytes would need to be sorted through. Judge Barbara Lynn then set a new trial date for February 21, 2017.

Looking back at the three guilty verdicts, it is interesting that all three were members of the inner circle. They, and only they, have paid the ultimate "Price." Their lives will be forever changed. They will always have a criminal record, a lifelong stain that can never be removed.

Sherman had more determination than almost anyone his new personal trainer Dan Judge had ever met. He knew that Sherman's left side had been paralyzed, but he began seeing progress. Sherman's left hand and leg began to show signs of improvement. Those signs of improvement came just as the Price trial was coming to a close.

Sherman had felt guilt about being disabled during the investigation, but his trainer taught him to let go of that guilt. Sherman stated, "Once I let go, I started improving. And now, I am free. I'm a different person now."

Would Sherman's oversight have made a difference in the John Wiley Price trial? The answer is yes, it would have. But Sherman bears no blame for its outcome.

CHAPTER 18

# Preparing for Trial

There is no question that Don Sherman carried a heavy burden of guilt for several years after suffering an almost-fatal stroke. He had been the FBI Special Agent in Charge. His track record had been perfect. The Price investigation would be different from all the others. Sherman knew that. Every item reviewed, every detail analyzed was thoroughly documented to the extent that there was more than one million files. All of that evidence was stored in Sherman's mind. Even after suffering a debilitating stroke, his mind remained sharp. He could recall every detail of the lengthy investigation.

In all fairness, he should feel no guilt for his untimely affliction. A couple of wheels on the government's train may have been off track, but the FBI on the other hand is a huge operation and should have been able to get its train back on track. In reality, that never happened. The operation seemed completely dependent upon one agent with personal knowledge of all details. Computers can store terabytes of information, but computers are not able to reason.

The trial would have likely started at least a year sooner had Sherman not been sidelined. It would have been before memories of witnesses had begun to fade. Once Sherman was sidelined, there was no one to guide prosecutors. No one to present his usual Chart of Evidence. Only he would have been able to do that. The jurors would normally have taken the chart into the jury room after the closing statements. The chart would have allowed them to follow the trail. Dozens of reporters, public officials and others, including myself, have asked how this trial could have gone so wrong.

It became apparent that there would be a trial once IRS and FBI agents fanned out across the Dallas area. They simultaneously served search warrants on the homes and offices of Kathy Nealy, Dapheny Fain, Karen Manning and John W. Price. It should have been no surprise to Price. He had known that he was under investigation ever since he sued me in 2009. The indictment for Price was extensive. It contained more than 100 pages. It appears that he faced at least thirteen charges.

Count one pertained to conspiracy to commit bribery. It pertained to a local government that receives federal funds. It specifically claimed that he was given a total of approximately $1 million in cash. He also received new cars and property that came from businesses that hired Nealy in order to provide influence. It claimed that Campbell helped facilitate that activity. I'm not sure why he was charged at the same time as Price, especially since Tantillo and Manning had been previously indicted.

Counts two through seven pertained to deprivation of services by mail fraud. It alleged that Price and Nealy were using the postal service in order to funnel money.

Count eight was for conspiracy to defraud the Internal Revenue Service. It claimed that Price failed to report income from business that he co-owned, sales of art and land deals. It also claimed that Nealy and Fain helped Price hide earnings. Those earnings were not reported.

Counts nine through eleven pertained to filing a false US income tax return. Years 2007 through 2009 were specifically mentioned.

Count twelve claims that Nealy tried to hide money that she gave Price. It claimed that she disguised the money as campaign contributions, charitable donations, real estate transactions, and luxury car purchases.

Count thirteen pertains to making a false statement. Agents reported that Fain had made a false statement during their investigation.

Nine charges total were brought against Kathy Nealy. It was always thought that she would be tried at a later date. The plan was reevaluated after Price's trial failed to gain traction. It is difficult to imagine, but she walked. She never went to trial.

Fain was charged with two counts, one for conspiracy to defraud the Internal Revenue Service and the other for making a false statement to federal agents. She was found not guilty on both charges. Almost no one ever escapes the charge of making a false statement to FBI agents.

Only one charge was levied against Campbell. He was charged with conspiracy to commit bribery. He entered a guilty plea and received probation.

The lion's share of charges went to Price. He faced eleven counts total. He was found not guilty on charges one through seven. Charges nine through eleven resulted in a hung jury. Jurors had deliberated for seven days total.

The entire trial lasted seven weeks. It was the first time that news reporters recall Judge Barbara Lynn chastising prosecutors in front of a jury. Many had covered all of her public corruption trials from Paul Fielding and Al Lipscomb to Don Hill. Many were wondering if jurors might be getting the impression that she was chastising DOJ officials, especially after she sternly admonished prosecutors for the fourth time in the presence of jurors.

Dallas public officials had been found guilty in every previous FBI corruption case. So what was different about this one? It appears that the consensus of opinion relates to one consistent fact. In the past the person accepting the bribe, along with the person making the bribe, had always been charged. There was no exception to this. The jury wasn't faced with handing out fair and equal punishment for only side of the deal. But there are also other facts to consider.

This case started out just like any other. The original complainant met with Department of Justice and FBI officials. Public corruption cases require upper management approval, all the way up to the Department of Justice officials in Washington, D.C. It is difficult to get a high-profile case approved. I initially doubted that they would take this case, but they did.

Most cases don't linger for ten years. But this investigation was far more complicated than others in the Dallas area. Previous cases were much narrower in focus. They usually involved one person, or one company, that was bribing one or more public officials. But then those officials had been in office for only a short period of time. This was not the situation with Price. He had been in office for more than twenty years by the time their investigation got underway.

Agents would follow the money in previous investigations. A signature on the back of a check was proof positive. And they would follow the money in this investigation, but then there were all of those automobiles that Price owned. It was reported that Price owned at least thirteen vintage automobiles. Agents felt that many of those collectible cars had been obtained through his association with a bail bond company owner. Almost none had a clear title. Titles had been obtained by means of a special hearing. All hearings were private. Records indicated that Dallas County Tax Assessor-Collector David Childs signed off on at least five titles during 2007. A canceled check, or other proof of ownership, is not required.

It was also reported that the investigation was becoming so complex that agents were instructed to narrow their focus. The previous targets were not experienced at hiding the money. Price was not just experienced at hiding the money, he was an expert. Agents probably would have never found his primary checking account except for his bragging. They discovered that the account wasn't even in his name. There was also the land that Price had bought from two different people, all in the same day—land that had originally been in the name of Danny Faulkner.

Special Agent in Charge Don Sherman was smart. He was also predictable. In the past he had generated new cases by spinning off from the original target. But so many cases were spinning off his main target that their focus had to be narrowed. This was not a simple case of bribery. Agents felt they knew how the cars tied in but eventually began to concentrate on following the money. Some agents felt that at least one public figure higher up the ladder was involved. But other investigations were boxed up and put on hold.

There seemed to be no money trail for the vintage cars. The U.S. Marshals Service did seize all funds from sale of the property. Agents also seized more than $220,000 in cash from a large safe found in Price's Oak Cliff home. One report indicated that the court ordered Price to pay $80,000 in legal fees. The court also ordered him to turn over any funds that might be floating around in some undiscovered account. And sure enough, one eventually turned up, according to a news article.

It would be three years after the 2011 raid on homes and offices of Price and his inner circle before a judge unsealed the lengthy indictment. On July 25, 2014, FBI agents arrested Price during the early morning hours while he was on his way to the office. Nealy was also arrested, and Fain was instructed to turn herself in. I'm not sure why he was arrested, since most high-profile defendants are usually allowed to surrender. News cameras were all over the place by the time Price walked out the door. His only comments were, "I did nothing wrong. I'm not guilty of anything. I knew this day would come."

U. S. Attorney Sarah Saldana held a press conference inside the Earl Cabell Federal Building. She made it clear that 109-page indictment had been unsealed. She then mentioned that Price had accepted more than $447,000 in cash and checks. She then added that there was an additional $200,000 for the sale of property. She also reported that he had received more than $191,000 for the use of a secretly purchased BMW convertible and a Chevrolet Avalanche pickup every two years for the last four years. That total included automobile insurance for both vehicles. She also said that Price violated his promise to uphold the law. It was reported that Price had $1,200 cash in his pocket at the time of his arrest. It was not disclosed if that money was returned.

Kathy Nealy was no longer driving the bus for high-level Dallas-area Democratic political figures seeking elected office. She would have previously been their first stop. That was before she became a cooperating witness in the Don Hill corruption case. She had risen from a struggling young widow to become known as the Champion Maker. And now the government had nine indictments against Nealy. It was thought that she would be on trial alongside Price and Dapheny Fain.

The government's strategy was falling apart. The plan was to have Price, Fain, and Nealy all in the courtroom at one time. Prosecutors would frequently mention that Nealy funneled money to Price. They claim she deposited checks and cash into his personal account. But she would not stand trial along with Price. Her attorneys claimed that she had been granted immunity during the Don Hill trial. They claimed that her immunity had never been revoked. Whether it had been or not, Judge Lynn ruled that she was exempt from testifying during Price's trial.

Nealy had agreed to be a consultant for James R. Fisher on the affordable-housing project. Fisher was originally the consultant for Dallas Mayor Pro-Tem Don Hill. But Hill then decided that he wanted to work with another developer by the name of Brian Potashnik. Nealy eventually admitted guilt in that case and agreed to testify for the government in exchange for leniency. Incidentally, that agreement was never put in writing. It was a verbal agreement. But it allowed her to escape prosecution in the Price bribery trial.

The government listed charges against four different individuals. One charge was levied against Campbell and two against Fain. Nealy had nine charges against her. The remaining thirteen charges were against Price. Campbell entered a guilty plea and Judge Barbara Lynn ruled that Kathy Nealy would be removed with instructions that she could be tried at a later date. That date never arrived. The only defendants in the courtroom were John Wiley Price and Dapheny Fain.

Price had the best defense attorneys that the taxpayers could buy. No question that they were good. They even asked the judge to admonish prosecutors for not including a photo of a parking decal. I'm not sure of its significance since there were more than a million files total in the case. But Judge Lynn did admonish prosecutors, and that set the tone for jurors' opinion of the government's prosecutors.

Lead prosecutor Walt Junker was in charge. This was a criminal case and needed a strong, experienced prosecutor. Junker had previously handled civil forfeiture cases in the U. S. Attorney's office. He was not experienced in high-profile criminal cases.

CHAPTER 19

# Wrapping It Up

There is no question that the majority of complaints pertaining to public corruption came during my first year in office. I received several during my first three months in office. Most were received during the first year of my four-year term. We have previously mentioned a county commissioner, two constables, and the district attorney. But in addition to the two constables, there is at least one other elected official whose improprieties I acknowledge being responsible for calling attention to.

The party chairwoman had publicly criticized me and stated that she would be glad when I was gone. It wasn't about Democrats or Republicans. I grew up being taught to always stand for what was right. Even if it was the opposition. And I believed elected officials were obligated to uphold their sacred oath of office.

It is interesting that the fabric of Dallas County government is interwoven with many of the same people in various capacities through the years. One year a person might be representing defendants, and a few years later they might be prosecuting for the government. Another person is selling a Dodge Viper to a county commissioner, and the next year he is a defendant in one of the largest savings and loan fraud cases in the United States.

Ted Lyon was serving as defense attorney for Dallas County Justice of the Peace Carlos Medrano in 2012. A few years later he was serving as special prosecutor in Constable Evans's trial. Judge Barbara Lynn was very strict during the Don Hill trial. She even chastised Hill and his attorney for speaking about the trial outside of court. She felt that he should be held in contempt for violating her gag order. The judge then appointed Terence Hart as special prosecutor in Don Hill's contempt of court investigation. Hart had served as lead prosecutor in the Danny Faulkner savings and loan trial in the 1980s.

Carlos Medrano unseated incumbent Oak Cliff Justice of the Peace Luis Sepulveda by 150 votes. I had a complainant in my office the next day. I ask for the proof and there was none. I explained that I needed proof. I then explained that a signed affidavit from the witnesses would certainly help. The complainant returned in about a week with stacks of signed and notarized complaints. It appeared to be a clear case of voter irregularities.

I instructed the complainant to make a copy of all documents and leave the originals with me. One of my devoted assistants spent several days researching each and every document before briefing me. There were various and numerous irregularities. Some appeared serious. Based on previous experience with our district attorney, I believed it would be a waste of time to present any of the evidence to the local district attorney's office. So, I headed to Austin once again.

This time, I was meeting with the secretary of state. I knew that the case would be handed over to the state AG if they decided to prosecute. I also knew that, in the past, approval was needed from the local DA before the AG could prosecute. If so, that would never happen. But there is a provision in the election code that allows cases involving voter fraud to be moved to a contiguous county.

Several weeks passed before I received official notice from the secretary of state that the case had been referred to the AG's office for prosecution. In the meantime Luis Sepulveda had sued Dallas County in an effort to have the election overturned. He was not successful, but additional allegations did surface during that trial. That information was turned over to investigators at the AG's office. A grand jury was impaneled in Rockwall County. Carlos Medrano was found guilty on a felony charge for illegally obtaining the vote of his niece. Her residence was in Mesquite, Texas. Not Oak Cliff.

Medrano was sentenced to 180 days in the Rockwall County jail, fined $2,500, and given five years probation. His attorney, Ted Lyon, stated that he would immediately appeal the guilty verdict. Medrano was suspended after being indicted. However, he continued to receive his $108,000 salary until being found guilty and removed from office. Sepulveda wanted his job back. It was reported that Price was adamantly opposed. I do know that Luis Sepulveda had frequently complained about the electronic traffic tickets.

It was shortly after Medrano's trial that commissioners decided to remove 32 deputy constables from the budget. They then added 32 positions to the sheriff's department.

The county budget director claimed that the county could save $190,000 per year by making the change. Constables claimed the reason was because several deputy constables had complained about being required to work without pay for Price's annual charity. The commissioners explained that it was all in the interest of saving money. Price's annual charity fest then became part of his public corruption trial.

*Carlos Medrano's Campaign Photo*

A frequently asked question continues to linger after a verdict was rendered in John Wiley Price's lengthy trial. What went wrong? That question has been asked over and over, time and time again. I do not claim to be an expert at rendering such an opinion. But I will attempt to give you a view based on following public corruption trials in the Dallas area. That involvement dates back to the Paul Fielding and Al Lipscomb trial.

Fielding had contacted me out of concern that his office phone calls were being monitored. I offered, as a favor, to stop by and take a look. Remember, I had been in the security business. My parting words to Fielding were "I didn't find anything in this office that indicates you are being monitored. But if the FBI is surveilling you, you'll never know it. That is all done from inside the telephone company's switching office. Does Al Lipscomb have an office here? I noticed a desk in the next office with his name tag on it." Fielding replied that someone placed a name tag on that desk as a joke. Of course, the rest is history.

Electronic "bugs" were extremely difficult to locate in those days. The only one that I recall finding was in the phone room of the Bob Dole for President campaign office at the Meadows Building. I asked the local campaign manager to follow me outside. Once outside, I explained that I had discovered what appears to be an electronic listening device. I advised that he go to another location and make a call to his head-quarters. Then I explained that the Secret Service will know exactly what to do. But I said to please make the call from another location.

I received a phone call the next day from an official with the secret service asking if the bug had been on the lower right panel board in the phone room. I explained that it was in that exact location. The agent responded, "Well, I wish the manager would have called us from another phone. It appears that someone overheard the call. The bug is dead. There is no way to trace a dead bug."

It is clear that FBI agents arrested Price in the 5500 block of Harry Hines Boulevard at 8:30 a.m. on July 25, 2014. Nealy was also arrested and Fain was instructed to turn herself in. All were released on bond later that day. Here is a summary of what I believe were some of the underlying problems. They are not listed in order of occurrence.

A. Failed to control jury selection.
B. No major co-conspirators indicted.

C. Nealy was not standing trial.

D. Sherman was not leading prosecutors.

E. Experienced federal prosecutor was essential.

F. Judge reprimanded prosecution.

G. High profile defense attorneys.

H. Length of time before going to trial.

The original FBI Special Agent in Charge was the notable Don Sherman when the investigation first got its traction. The Dallas office had received a green light from its headquarters in Washington, D.C. Sherman was experienced at spinning new cases off his current target. The department was soon overwhelmed. New cases were stacking up faster than agents could investigate. It is reported that other agents were quietly brought in from other offices.

It soon appeared as if the case was stalled. Then the order came down to condense the investigation and to go after only what is needed to bring the commissioner to trial—in other words, to start following the money. It was thought that the rest would take care of itself. Following the money was difficult in the beginning. Price had years of experience. He knew how to hide the money. Some of the funds were in the form of land or automobiles. Some of the accounts were difficult to locate, and his primary checking account was not in his name. The transactions were numerous. Multiple players were involved. In addition to Price, there was Kathy Nealy, Daphney Fain and Karen Manning.

Now we understand why FBI investigators wanted to know about the women in Price's life. It would appear that only the women were trusted with his money. Price did ask the government to return all of the cash that agents confiscated from his residence.

He also wanted the funds that were seized for the property sale. But Judge Rene Toliver said, in essence, not so fast Mr. Price. There was this matter of his legal bill. He owed the government for his defense. The judge added, "I am aware of your financial status. Your collection of antique automobiles. You also own a house that you are renting to your son. You have a 2005 Bentley parked in the garage. Regardless of your status or office, you are required to pay your part."

The cash removed from Price's pockets would also go toward his legal fees. The judge did agree that the $20,000 ring, other jewelry, and a collection of expensive watches would be returned to Price. She said, "They can be sold in order to raise money to pay necessary living expenses." The appraisal for those items came in at $200,000 during trial. Fain was ordered to pay the government $114,000 in legal fees. Shirley Baccus-Lobel had requested a closed hearing. She told the judge that some of the information was sensitive. Judge Toliver responded, "I am not going to clear the courtroom."

Baccus-Lobel told the judge that Price was at the end of his ability to earn money. She also mentioned he had debts to pay. The judge responded, "There were plenty of able-bodied attorneys to pick from. He could have chosen any of them."

Many feel that Price wanted the most expensive attorney money could buy. Before trial, he was more concerned about the price of his freedom. It is not clear how much of the total cost Price paid toward his defense team. His defense team did pay off in the long run. It was able to get government witnesses to admit that they really did not know what the payments to Price were for and that they did not know the exact extent of the relationship between Nealy, Price, and his chief of staff, Dapheny Fain.

Chad Meacham was the attorney originally responsible for gaining immunity for Kathy Nealy. It was during the Don Hill federal corruption case that he asked for her immunity. Meacham said in an interview that the agreement was oral and that it was never in writing, and he could not understand why any judge would have allowed it to carry forward. Meacham also felt that prosecutors lost considerable favor with the jury over letting Nealy walk. He has doubts that Nealy will ever be prosecuted or held accountable for any of her wrongdoing.

Defense attorney and former public defender for the government, Clint Broden, was very critical of the lead prosecutor. He stated, "Walt Junker previously handled the civil forfeiture cases in the U.S. Attorney's office. And now here he is running the biggest case they've had."

Radio talk show host and long-time loyal Price supporter Robert Ashley said, "There are many that believe this is selective prosecution. What about the white guys that gave him the money? They knew where that money was going. I didn't see any white guys indicted in this case." Dallas attorney Victor Vital says the government had more than 1,000 items to enter as evidence. There was no way a juror could remember all of that. Whoever had the simplest explanation would win the case. Vital also stated, "Price could win this case if he stays off the stand and keeps his mouth shut. If he gets on the stand and starts talking, then it's all over."

Ashley was right about one thing. Price had developed a loyal following over thirty years ago. Those that are still living remain loyal to this day. It does not matter what he may, or may not, be charged with. Even if arrested, they will always follow Price. Ashley calls them his loyal supporters.

Almost ten years would pass from the onset of his initial

investigation until a verdict was reached. That's an unusually long time. Previous white-collar cases in the Dallas area moved along at a much more rapid pace. Once a trial date was set, defense attorneys were required to turn over discovery. They claimed that the government had spent years building a false case against Price. They were not required to prove their claims. The government does have to prove its allegations beyond a reasonable doubt.

It appeared that defense attorneys were in charge of jury selection. It is true that the courthouse was in downtown Dallas, but this was a federal court. It represents the Northern District of Texas. Jurors could have been selected from Rockwall, Johnson, Ellis, Hunt, or Navarro counties. All of the outlying areas are more conservative than Dallas County. Potential jurors had been mailed a twenty-page questionnaire with instructions to complete it and bring it along with them once the trial was underway. It was headline news on all the local radio and TV stations.

U.S. District Judge Barbara Lynn said that the seventy-member panel was the largest gathering of potential jurors that had ever assembled in her courtroom. She then started off the voir dire process by explaining to the panel that in Texas it is pronounced "vore dire." She then explained to panel members, "This case has generated and will continue to generate a lot of publicity. Nothing you have read, heard, or seen has anything to do with this case. This case will be decided in this room, by evidence and testimony heard in this room."

U.S. Assistant Attorney Walt Junker would then take over the voir dire. It is important to realize that the government had no expert, or anyone else, that specialized in jury selection. He seemed to stumble a few times with his line of questioning. Price had been pre-warned to hold back his remarks and comments.

He was observed quickly grabbing a notepad and frantically beginning to scribble a message to one of his attorneys. Junker had asked the panel if they would need a smoking gun to convict Price.

He then addressed individual jurors. The issue of race seemed to be a common thread as he moved from one potential juror to another. He then called on panel member number 67. He asked 67 if he thought race would be an issue in this trial. The panel member was an African-American attorney. He responded with, "As soon as I saw you addressing all your questions about race to African-American women, I knew it was going to be an issue."

One of Junker's most serious mistakes was probably asking panel members how they would feel about convicting Price for bribery when none of the people that bribed him were on trial. That could have really tainted some potential jurors before the trial even got underway.

Defense Attorney Shirley Baccus-Lobel then took over the voir dire. It was as if a switch had been flipped. The entire process changed in an instant. Sitting at the table with Price and his two prominent attorneys was an expert in jury selection. She knew how to navigate the system. She was an expert in selecting jurors that would render a verdict in favor of the side she was hired to represent. She knew how to accomplish her mission without the opposition even being aware of what was happening.

It was announced early on that the jury would not be sequestered. Putting a jury up in a hotel room no longer serves the purpose it once did. Hotels now have cable television, high-speed internet, and all the other conveniences of home. The jury selection was completed in just eight hours. It had been estimated that the process would take up to a week. Attorneys for the defense were delighted. The prosecution was also happy to see that the selection process was over. But it appears that the defense had fared much better with the selection.

Judge Lynn instructed the remaining panel to go home. She told them to call the jury information system at 10:00 p.m. that night. They would then find out if they had been selected as a juror at that time. Price sat facing the potential jurors during the entire process. He didn't seem at all concerned or nervous. It was if he knew that his team (he liked using that word) had it all under control. And they did.

The defense team was good. They showed emotion. They could even be dramatic—sometimes, a little too dramatic. The prosecution was completely without emotion. It was if they were presenting a chart on last year's change in the population of an ant farm.

Once the trial was underway, Special Agent in Charge Diego Rodriguez addressed jurors. "The FBI's top criminal program priority is investigating allegations of public corruption. The defendants' alleged actions were designed for personal financial gain at the expense of their constituents and the federal government. These types of actions constitute a breach of the public's trust, erode confidence in government, and cost taxpayers money and resources," he told the court.

All of this was good information, but there was no Don Sherman evidence chart. Where was the personal emotion that was always there when the previous SAIC was leading the case? Sherman agreed to testify as a witness for the prosecution. It was a mistake that he would later regret. Defense attorney Tom Mills was standing outside of the courthouse when Sherman walked by. Sherman looked over at Mills and said, "Hello Bill. How are you?" He knew immediately that Mills would probably use that against him. But it was too late. He had already spoken. It was the second day of trial. Mills wasted no time in dressing down Sherman. He claimed that his memory was failing. Mills explained how he didn't recall his name. He mentioned that Sherman depended on a cane just to walk across the floor.

I reluctantly also agreed to testify for the government. I was reluctant not because I didn't know details but because I knew that the defense would try to make me look like the bad guy. And I was right. Lead defense attorney Shirley Baccus-Lobel started off with some routine questions. "Mr. Foster, can you tell the court the names and district number of each commissioner during the period of time that you served as county judge?" she asked. I went down the list starting with district one.

The line of questioning then seemed to turn into badgering. The court took a lunch break. I walked over to my hotel for lunch. At one time it appeared that an unknown man was following me. So I decided to cross the street. He then crossed the street. This continued for several blocks. He stopped at the front entrance once I reached the hotel.

On returning from lunch, attorneys for both the prosecution and defense approached me. One of the defense attorneys wanted to know if I had talked to a former Dallas County employee in the courthouse lobby during lunch break. I answered in the affirmative. They then wanted to know her name and what we discussed. "Sorry, I do not recall her name. The conversation with her was brief. I told her I was headed to the hotel for lunch and wished her a good day," I responded. At that point, it became clear that their mystery man had followed me during the lunch break. Did they want to know whom I might be meeting? I was surprised that he didn't report back about the banana and low sugar protein drink I had for lunch.

Mills then wanted to know if I had been on an elevator with some of the jury members. "If you recall a deputy marshal kept watch over me in a conference room, I was not allowed into the courtroom until they were ready for me to take the stand," I said. "My back faces the jury and I cannot identify any one juror. No one on that elevator was wearing a jury ID badge." They seemed disappointed but appeased.

I was then back on the stand and Baccus-Lobel continued her badgering. She made the mistake of asking if a mayor had contacted me during the early days of the inland port disagreement. I responded that several mayors had called. I mentioned that I had met with and conversed with various mayors. She kept badgering. She wanted to know if I recalled meeting with an important mayor.

She then took a different approach. "What can you tell us about a meeting you had with Commissioner Price and Senator West?" she asked.

"I was headed home late one Friday evening when I received a call from Senator West. He wanted to know if I could stop by his office. I told him that I would be there shortly. Commissioner Price was standing in the lobby when I walked through the door. Senator West wanted me to place the item pertaining to the inland port back on the agenda. I explained that I had no intention of doing so. The senator became angry, began banging his fist on his desk. I got up and left. They then requested Mayor Leppert to call me. He wanted me to place the port item back on the agenda."

"Mr. Foster, please tell me how you know that Senator West asked the mayor to call you," she responded.

"The mayor started off the conversation with, 'Judge Foster, Senator West asked me to call you,'" I stated before promptly being interrupted.

Baccus-Lobel suddenly changed the subject. It appeared that she had asked a question that she didn't know the answer to.

Jim Schultze of the *Dallas Observer* reported that it was now clear for the first time that Dallas Mayor Leppert was directly involved in delaying progress of the inland port project.

Baccus-Lobel continued pressing me for answers. "Mr. Foster, you stated earlier that an additional study of land use would delay the project. Can you tell me how that would have delayed the project?" she asked.

"Yes, the developer told me that he had signed deals with several major corporations that were ready to move into the project. The additional eighteen-month study killed those deals," I replied.

"Well, then Mr. Foster, can you name any of those major corporations?" she quickly demanded.

I began to reply with, "Yes, I know the name of several. The first one that comes to mind was Whirlpool, then there was . . ." Before I could get speak another word, she quickly interrupted. "Okay, thank you Mr. Foster. Your Honor, I have no more questions for this witness," she said. My testimony was finished.

I headed toward the courtroom exit. A deputy marshal met me at the door. He then requested that I follow him over to a nearby office. I was then handed an airline ticket. It was then back to the hotel for a quick checkout. They gave me exactly two and a half hours to get out of town. I was relieved that no one would be following me once aboard the plane. I have always wondered who they thought might have been meeting me.

I have always felt they were disappointed that I didn't have a secret meeting with some high-profile official. My only purpose was to tell the truth and let the court know what I had experienced.

Jim Schutze reported the following day that my testimony did serious damage for the defense. He went on to report that they just kept asking all the wrong questions.

Some of the questions appeared to have originated from Price. His attorneys were not around back in those days. The majority of their questions did backfire. But in the end, it was not enough to change the mind of one or more jurors.

Defense attorneys may have made another step in the wrong direction while asking Allen Wilson, the FBI's lead agent on the case, about a 2005 subpoena. He was asked why the FBI didn't investigate Price and Nealy back in 2005. Defense attorneys then stated that you were looking at their records back then.

Wilson replied that the 2005 subpoena was for Nealy's involvement in the Don Hill bribery trial. It was clear back then Price and Nealy were exchanging funds, he stated.

Wilson then added, "The confidential Dallas County documents Price leaked to Nealy, to help her clients, came to light in later years. It was the cornerstone of the bribery investigation. It was part of the access and influence Price provided Nealy to help her clients."

One concern after another seemed to arise about U.S. District Court Judge Barbara Lynn admonishing the prosecution in front of jurors—not once, but on four different occasions. No one seemed to recall her doing that previously. As the trial got closer to ending, the incidents seemed to be more frequent. Her frustration seemed to center around prosecuting attorneys not turning over evidence to defense attorneys in a timely fashion.

For some reason a comment the judge made about the charge of mail fraud keeps running through my mind. One of the charges against Price was mail fraud. Judge Lynn was very unhappy with the government's handling of that charge. The judge had been quoted as saying, "If the jury returns a guilty verdict for mail fraud, I will overturn that verdict. The government has not proved their charge of mail fraud. Once the verdicts were read, Price had been found not guilty on mail fraud.

The fourth incident involved a complaint from defense attorneys as the trial was nearing an end. Walt Junker replied that it was due to the volume of evidence, which seemed to really anger Lynn. The judge said that she saw a pattern there. When defense attorneys complained, Walt Junker left the courtroom and tried to track down the missing files. Once again I am guessing that members of the jury are not at all impressed.

Lynn told the jury about the latest incident. She then stated that she will give defense attorneys a wide leeway to introduce evidence from the newly revealed documents, without challenges from the government.

Jim Schultz told me a couple of days after the trial ended that the case failed because the prosecution did a terrible job. It appears, at least in the eyes of the judge, that he was right.

Going back in time for a couple of minutes: A high profile raid of the homes and offices of Price, Nealy, Fain, and Manning by FBI and IRS agents had made national news. It appeared that the case was finally moving forward. Two of Price's business associates—Pettis Norman, former football player for the Dallas Cowboys, and Jon Edmonds—were subpoenaed to testify before the federal grand jury. Their presence indicates how far back the investigation was reaching. Their involvement dated back to 2003. They, along with Price, were part of a group known as SALT. South Dallas Congresswoman Eddie Bernice Johnson claimed the group was trying to shake down a large land developer in southern Dallas County.

One reporter told me during the trial that he felt progress would have been better served by going to trial early on. He believes Price should have been indicted as soon as they had two or three solid charges. He also pointed out that agents wasted their time building a case against Fain and Nealy. Fain was never convicted, and Nealy never went to trial. Of course, hindsight is 20-20.

And what about all those business owners who were providing the payments? They were always indicted in the past. Why was this one different? Was it because the Perot family was involved? No one has been able to answer that question. But it would have had to be playing on the minds of jurors as they sat in their elevated jury box day after day, week after week.

Michael Berry had joined Hillwood, a Perot Company, in 1988. That was the year ground was broken for Alliance Airport in Tarrant County. Berry, Hillwood's president, would testify for the government. He believed that the development in southern Dallas County would be in direct competition with Alliance.

Alliance was in the process of expanding its runway for larger planes headed to Asia. It was also expanding its roads and enlarging its rail terminal. It needed government funds for all those projects. Berry then testified that he was worried that the rail carrier BNSF would move its cargo facility to southern Dallas County, since it had acquired land there. He also mentioned that BNSF officials had already told him that they would likely have to move.

Union Pacific already had its own facility at the inland port in southern Dallas County. It was Nealy's job to convince Price to delay the project. It was that simple. It appears they knew where the money was going. As mentioned earlier, Berry wanted Price to put a bar in the spokes of that wheel.

Hillwood's recently retired attorney, David Newsom, would then testify. He told the jury that he had recommended Hillwood hire Nealy in 2006. She could then gain Price's help in order to delay the project. Newsom said that he first met Nealy in the 1990s. He needed her help in seeking support from City of Dallas officials for their Victory development. The large development was anchored by American Airlines Center. Newsom then testified that he knew Nealy was close to Price and he knew that the inland port project was in Price's district.

The next item that he testified about is the one that caused Mayor Leppert, Senator West, and Commissioner Price to become angry with me. Newsom wanted land in DeSoto, Texas, to be included in the boundaries of the inland port. He knew it would require the approval of Commissioners Court. He believed that Nealy, through access to Price, could get him that approval. The project had already been approved by the DFW Airport's Board of Directors. Adding additional land would delay the project and require it be again submitted to the board for review.

It appears that Hillwood officials wanted the project killed. To me that would have been the "smoking gun" that defense attorneys were asking for. As time went on, those same officials wanted to become part of the project. Instead of hiring someone to kill the deal, they were constructing new office and warehouse space onsite.

You can imagine the jury's dilemma. The government is going after the man that took the money and the bribes. All the white men paying those bribes and providing the money were of no interest to the prosecution. There was also growing concern that the government was only prosecuting African Americans. Christian Campbell does appear to be the only white person indicted in this case.

We will never know what the FBI did or did not investigate. I do know that agents were very concerned about Price's antique, or vintage, car collection. They were also interested in any control that he, or any other public official, had over the bail bond board. Some deputy constables also met with federal agents. One of the concerns expressed by at least one deputy was any potential kickback money from the towing company. There were numerous complaints about deputies being required to work off duty, without pay, for Price's annual charity event. No indictment included those allegations. He was charged with tax evasion, though, for not reporting the income from those events.

Fain was found not guilty of lying to federal agents. She was also acquitted on a charge of helping Price hide money from the IRS. The jury was unable to reach a verdict on Price's charge of tax evasion. He was never retried on that charge. It would be difficult at this point to take Kathy Nealy to trial after Price was found not guilty on the same charges filed against her.

As we reach an end to just about everything that could be said pertaining to this subject, I look back in amazement. I sometimes wonder about my predecessors. Was it that they didn't care? I seriously doubt that they were that naive. Only they can answer that question. I have a couple theories on the subject, though.

Price was under investigation for years. I always wondered why wiretaps were not used in his investigation. They had been used in previous Dallas corruption cases, but not during the Price investigation. I do know that Price was already working with an attorney when he sued me. As a result of that lawsuit, he discovered that he was under federal investigation. He likely found a new lawyer at that point. My theory is that it was the attorney-client relationship that nixed the wiretaps. Or was it that Price was talking to some high-profile officials? I can't tell you if the commissioner, state senator, and mayor working together to kill a logistics hub was a crime or not. But I can tell you that it does not pass the smell test.

I did discover that there were wiretaps of both Price and Nealy during the 2005 Don Hill corruption investigation. Price was not charged in that case, but Nealy was. She later agreed to testify for the prosecution.

Price avoided jail. Yes, I know he spent a few hours being processed on the sixteenth floor of the Earl Cabell Federal Building in downtown Dallas after his arrest. There are various estimates as to his actual outlay of cash as a result of his arrest and trial. Those estimates vary. Some believe that his total cost tips the scale at $1.2 million. Let's hope that vendors are no longer lined up with a blank check.

I seriously doubt that any other elected official in Dallas County has been in office longer than John Wiley Price. He has been in that position since January 1, 1985. So, is he bulletproof? Is there a way to get him out of office? The roster containing his former opponents is lengthy. They all failed.

But I believe he has finally overdone it with his self-confidence. It was a bold move for Price to agree that the boundary for District Three would take in virtually half of Dallas County. But he did. And it does.

I also believe that a good challenger could unseat Price during his next election, especially now that Dallas County has a by-the-book Elections Administrator.

And, yes, I know just the person that I believe could do that. If he does decide to, his name on the ballot would be printed simply as Jim Foster.

Made in the USA
Monee, IL
01 June 2022

6714f865-f069-4584-b4f2-0e3ff0dab8deR01